Marko Lüftenegger
Martin Daumiller
Ingrid Schoon
(Editors)

COVID-19 and Coping With Future Crises

Perspectives of Educational and Developmental Psychology

Zeitschrift für Psychologie
Volume 231 / Number 3 / 2023

Library of Congress Cataloging in Publication information is available via the Library of Congress Marc Database under the LC Control Number 2023941738

© 2023 Hogrefe Publishing

Hogrefe Publishing
Incorporated and registered in the Commonwealth of Massachusetts, USA, and in Göttingen, Lower Saxony, Germany

No part of this publication may be reproduced, stored in a retrieval system or transmitted, in any form or by any means, electronic, mechanical, photocopying, microfilming, recording or otherwise, without written permission from the publisher.

Cover image ©iStock/valentinrussanov

Printed and bound in Germany

ISBN 978-0-88937-640-3

The *Zeitschrift für Psychologie*, founded by Hermann Ebbinghaus and Arthur König in 1890, is the oldest psychology journal in Europe and the second oldest in the world. Since 2007, it appears in English and is devoted to publishing topical issues that provide convenient state-of-the-art compilations of research in psychology, each covering an area of current interest.

The *Zeitschrift für Psychologie* is available as a journal in print and online by annual subscription and the different topical compendia are also available as individual titles by ISBN.

Editor-in-Chief	Michael Bošnjak, University of Trier, Department of Psychology, Universitätsring 15, 54296 Trier, Germany, +49 651 201 2706, bosnjak@uni-trier.de
Associate Editors	Benjamin E. Hilbig, Landau, Germany Andrea Kiesel, Freiburg, Germany Iris-Tatjana Kolassa, Ulm, Germany Steffi Pohl, Berlin, Germany Barbara Schober, Vienna, Austria Birgit Schyns, Reims, France Christiane Spiel, Vienna, Austria Elsbeth Stern, Zurich, Switzerland
Editorial Board	André Bittermann, Trier, Germany Susanne Braun, Durham, UK Tom Buchanan, London, UK Tanja Burgard, Trier, Germany Hanna Christiansen, Marburg, Germany Aleksandra Cichocka, Kent, UK Martin Daumiller, Augsburg, Germany Andreas Fischer, Heidelberg, Germany Biljana Gjoneska, Skopje, North Macedonia Andrew Gloster, Basel, Switzerland Mario Gollwitzer, Munich, Germany Rainer Greifeneder, Basel, Switzerland Tina Hascher, Bern, Switzerland Qiwei-Britt He, Princeton, NJ, USA Roland Imhoff, Mainz, Germany Olivier Klein, Brussels, Belgium Laura König, Bayreuth, Germany Goran Knezevic, Belgrade, Serbia Ljiljana Lazarevic, Belgrade, Serbia Ulrike Lueken, Berlin, Germany Marko Lüftenegger, Vienna, Austria Pedro Neves, Lisbon, Portugal Steffi Pohl, Berlin, Germany Ulf-Dietrich Reips, Konstanz, Germany Melanie Sauerland, Maastricht, The Netherlands Ingrid Schoon, London, UK Katariina Salmela-Aro, Helsinki, Finland Ingrid Schoon, London, UK Birgit Schyns, Reims, France Holger Steinmetz, Trier, Germany Jana Strahler, Freiburg, Germany Heta Tuominen, Helsinki, Finland Mathias Twardawski, Munich, Germany Esther Ulitzsch, Kiel, Germany Nadine Wedderhoff, Neuruppin, Germany
Publisher	Hogrefe Publishing, Merkelstr. 3, 37085 Göttingen, Germany, Tel. +49 551 999 50 0, Fax +49 551 999 50 425, publishing@hogrefe.com North America: Hogrefe Publishing Corporation, 44 Merrimac Street, Suite 207, Newburyport, MA 01950, USA, Tel. +1 978 255 3700, customersupport@hogrefe.com
Production	Irina Rau, Hogrefe Publishing, Merkelstr. 3, 37085 Göttingen, Germany, Tel. +49 551 999 50 430, Fax +49 551 999 50 425, production@hogrefe.com
Subscriptions	Hogrefe Publishing, Herbert-Quandt-Str. 4, 37081 Göttingen, Germany, Tel. +49 551 999 50 900, Fax +49 551 999 50 998
Advertising/Inserts	Hogrefe Publishing, Merkelstr. 3, 37085 Göttingen, Germany, Tel. +49 551 999 50 423, Fax +49 551 999 50 425, marketing@hogrefe.com
ISSN	ISSN-L 2151-2604, ISSN-Print 2190-8370, ISSN-Online 2151-2604
Copyright Information	© 2023 Hogrefe Publishing. This journal as well as the individual contributions and illustrations contained within it are protected under international copyright law. No part of this publication may be reproduced, stored in a retrieval system, or transmitted, in any form or by any means, electronic, mechanical, photocopying, microfilming, recording or otherwise, without prior written permission from the publisher. All rights, including translation rights, reserved.
Publication	Published in 4 topical issues per annual volume.
Subscription Prices	Calendar year subscriptions only. Rates for 2023: Institutions - from US $353.00 / € 272.00 (print only; pricing for online access can be found in the journals catalog at hgf.io/journalscatalog); Individuals US $208.00 / €149.00 (all plus US $18.00 / €16.80 shipping & handling; €12.80 in Germany). Single issue US $49.00 / € 34.95 (plus shipping & handling).
Payment	Payment may be made by check, international money order, or credit card, to Hogrefe Publishing, Merkelstr. 3, 37085 Göttingen, Germany. US and Canadian subscriptions can also be ordered from Hogrefe Publishing Corporation, 44 Merrimac Street, Suite 207, Newburyport, MA 01950, USA, Tel. +1 978 255 3700, customersupport@hogrefe.com
Electronic Full Text	The full text of *Zeitschrift für Psychologie* is available online at https://econtent.hogrefe.com and in PsycARTICLES™.
Abstracting Services	Abstracted/indexed in Current Contents/Social and Behavioral Sciences (CC/S&BS), Social Sciences Citation Index (SSCI), Research Alert, PsycINFO, PASCAL, PsycLit, IBZ, IBR, ERIH, and PSYNDEX. Impact Factor (2022): 1.8 2022 Impact Factor 1.8, 5-year Impact Factor 2.3, *Journal Citation Reports* (Clarivate 2023)

Contents

Editorial	Navigating the Pandemic and Future Crises: Insights From Developmental and Educational Psychology *Marko Lüftenegger, Martin Daumiller, and Ingrid Schoon*	**175**
Review Article	How Did COVID-19 Affect Education and What Can Be Learned Moving Forward? A Systematic Meta-Review of Systematic Reviews and Meta-Analyses *Martin Daumiller, Raven Rinas, Ingrid Schoon, and Marko Lüftenegger*	**177**
Original Articles	Comparison of Parent-Rated Teaching Activities During the First and Second School Lockdowns and Its Association With Students' Learning Outcomes During Distant Teaching *Ricarda Steinmayr, Rebecca Lazarides, Linda Wirthwein, and Hanna Christiansen*	**192**
	Changes in Teachers' Perceptions of School Quality During COVID-19: Findings From a Longitudinal Study Based on Propensity Score Balancing *Christoph Helm and Stephan Gerhard Huber*	**204**
	Navigating an Uncertain Future: How Schools Can Support Career Adaptability of Young People in the Aftermath of the COVID-19 Pandemic *Ingrid Schoon and Golo Henseke*	**217**
	The Role of Basic Need Satisfaction for Motivation and Self-Regulated Learning During COVID-19: A Longitudinal Study *Elisabeth Rosa Pelikan, Luisa Grützmacher, Katharina Hager, Julia Holzer, Selma Korlat, Martin Mayerhofer, Barbara Schober, Christiane Spiel, and Marko Lüftenegger*	**228**
Erratum	Correction to Christiansen & Lueken, 2023	**239**

Editorial

Navigating the Pandemic and Future Crises

Insights From Developmental and Educational Psychology

Marko Lüftenegger[1,2], Martin Daumiller[3], and Ingrid Schoon[4,5]

[1]Centre of Teacher Education, University of Vienna, Austria
[2]Department of Developmental and Educational Psychology, Faculty of Psychology, University of Vienna, Austria
[3]Department of Psychology, University of Augsburg, Germany
[4]Berlin Social Science Center, Germany
[5]Institute of Education (IoE), University College London (UCL), University of London, UK

I have thought a lot and I am a different person now. My view of the world has changed and I have found myself. (Secondary school student from Austria reflecting on the pandemic after the third lockdown, April 2021)

COVID-19 has challenged societies and our educational systems in particular, with dramatic changes to established practices and imposing new challenges. As a consequence, vast differences emerged in how individual students, teachers, and parents, different schools, and different educational systems managed to cope with this unprecedented crisis. As we can see from the quote of the student above, some individuals succeeded in this endeavor, but many others did not. The scientific community quickly responded to the crisis with a surge of pandemic-related studies and research papers, also broader known as the "COVID-ization" of research (Brainard, 2022). This global shift of attention by researchers helped to fill knowledge gaps but also produced many poor-quality studies as many researchers worked outside of their main expertise and less rigorous peer review processes allowed for rapid dissemination of knowledge. Recent publication trends showed that these increased publication activities decreased together with the decreasing severity of the pandemic (Brainard, 2022) while many meta-analyses and systematic literature reviews emerged (Daumiller et al., 2023).

From our perspective, this is now a good time to focus on what we can learn from this global pandemic and ensuing economic crisis and how to support educational policies in steering and mitigating such crises in the future. This topical issue brings together current research on the effects of the pandemic and possible coping mechanisms from both developmental and educational psychology perspectives – a promising combination to focus on the effects of various phases of the educational career (Spiel et al., 2022). Following a systematic meta-review on the existing state of research and research deficits, this topical issue entails four empirical papers with longitudinal designs investigating parents, teachers, adolescents, and university students from Austria, Germany, and the United Kingdom.

This topical issue starts off with a systematic meta-review by Daumiller and colleagues (2023, this issue), which focuses on the effects that the pandemic had on education as a whole. The review brings together evidence on multiple topics (including school closures, e-teaching and learning, mental and physical health), populations (students, teachers, parents), and levels of education. The summary and evaluation of 55 systematic reviews and meta-analyses published until November 2022 provide a comprehensive narrative of how the pandemic affected education and what can be learned moving forward while highlighting the challenges and opportunities of research during such crises.

Turning to the empirical papers, Steinmayr and colleagues (2023, this issue) investigate whether distant teaching activities increased between school lockdowns during the second quarter of 2020 and the first quarter of 2021 and whether the frequency of distant teaching activities was related to students' outcomes during distant learning. Relying on a large sample of German parents, the authors concluded that distant teaching activities greatly increased between the school lockdowns. However, distant teaching activities varied strongly in both elementary and secondary schools. Moreover, distant teaching activities, children's characteristics, and social background were independently related to students' outcomes (motivation, competent and independent learning, perceived learning progress).

In the third paper, Helm and Huber (2023, this issue) explore the effects of the pandemic on school quality in a longitudinal study (between 2016 and autumn 2020) with a large sample of German school teachers. The authors consider different aspects of school quality such as school climate, collective teacher efficacy, teacher cooperation, and distributed leadership. Using multiple-group multiple-indicator univariate latent change score modeling, they largely did not find differences in the development of teachers' perceptions of school quality during the pandemic compared to developments that occurred prior to the pandemic. Notable exceptions are adaptive teaching which increased more than before the pandemic and social support between teachers which decreased more than before the pandemic.

The fourth paper by Schoon and Henseke (2023, this issue) draws on a nationally representative study (YEAH) of 16- to 25-year-olds conducted in the United Kingdom between February 2021 and June 2022 to investigate if school-based career preparation activities can support the development of career adaptability of young people in the aftermath of the COVID-19 pandemic. The authors show that career adaptability is malleable and confirm the importance of school-based career preparation activities in supporting adaptive career-related cognitions and life satisfaction in times of economic uncertainty and upheaval. This is a crucial finding as young people have to navigate an increasingly uncertain and precarious employment market.

The issue concludes with a paper by Pelikan and colleagues (2023, this issue) who explore longitudinal effects between university students' satisfaction of their basic psychological needs (competence, autonomy, and social relatedness), intrinsic motivation, and self-regulated learning using a cross-lagged panel model. Findings from a large sample with four waves between April 2020 and July 2021 showed that surprisingly all measured constructs remained stable. The satisfaction of basic needs was cross-sectionally related to intrinsic motivation. The authors did not find cross-lagged effects on intrinsic motivation. Furthermore, self-regulated learning showed small but significant cross-lagged positive effects on intrinsic motivation at all waves, suggesting an important role of self-regulated learning in shaping intrinsic motivation during the introduction of distance learning.

Each of the five articles contributes to a better understanding of the COVID-19 pandemic's effects on different aspects of the education system. Moreover, the findings encourage further research on how to cope with future crises as more scientific knowledge is necessary to inform theory, politics, and practice.

References

Brainard, J. (2022). 'COVID-ization' of research levels off. *Science*, *376*(6595), 782–783. https://doi.org/10.1126/science.add0532

Daumiller, M., Rivas, R., Schoon, I., & Lüftenegger, M. (2023). How did COVID-19 affect education and what can be learned moving forward? A systematic meta-review of systematic reviews and meta-analyses. *Zeitschrift für Psychologie*, *231*(3), 177–191. https://doi.org/10.1027/2151-2604/a000527

Helm, C., & Huber, S. (2023). Changes in teachers' perceptions of school quality during COVID-19. *Zeitschrift für Psychologie*, *231*(3), 204–216. https://doi.org/10.1027/2151-2604/a000529

Pelikan, E., Grützmacher, L., Hager, K., Holzer, J., Korlat, S., Mayerhofer, M., Schober, B., Spiel, C., & Lüftenegger, M. (2023). The role of basic need satisfaction for motivation and self-regulated learning during COVID-19: A longitudinal study. *Zeitschrift für Psychologie*, *231*(3), 228–238. https://doi.org/10.1027/2151-2604/a000531

Schoon, I., & Henseke, G. (2023). Navigating an uncertain future: How schools can support career adaptability of young people in the aftermath of the Covid-19 pandemic. *Zeitschrift für Psychologie*, *231*(3), 217–227. https://doi.org/10.1027/2151-2604/a000530

Spiel, C., Götz, T., Wagner, P., Lüftenegger, M., & Schober, B. (Eds.). (2022). *Bildungspsychologie: Eine Einführung* [Educational Psychology: An Introduction]. Hogrefe. https://doi.org/10.1026/03108-000

Steinmayr, R., Lazarides, R., Wirthwein, L., & Christiansen, H. (2023). Comparison of parent-rated teaching activities during the first and second school lockdown and its association with students' learning outcomes during distant teaching. *Zeitschrift für Psychologie*, *231*(3), 192–203. https://doi.org/10.1027/2151-2604/a000528

Published online July 18, 2023

Acknowledgments
Many thanks also go to the anonymous expert reviewers who gave constructive criticism and detailed feedback.

Marko Lüftenegger
Center for Teacher Education
University of Vienna
Porzellangasse 4
1090 Wien
Austria
marko.lueftenegger@univie.ac.at

Review Article

How Did COVID-19 Affect Education and What Can Be Learned Moving Forward?

A Systematic Meta-Review of Systematic Reviews and Meta-Analyses

Martin Daumiller[1], Raven Rinas[1], Ingrid Schoon[2,3], and Marko Lüftenegger[4,5]

[1]Department of Psychology, University of Augsburg, Germany
[2]Berlin Social Science Center, Germany
[3]Institute of Education, University College London, University of London, UK
[4]Centre of Teacher Education, University of Vienna, Austria
[5]Department of Developmental and Educational Psychology, Faculty of Psychology, University of Vienna, Austria

Abstract: The COVID-19 pandemic drastically impacted the educational sector on a global front. A plethora of research has been conducted to better understand the effects that the pandemic had on education as a whole, including investigations into different topics (e.g., school closures, e-teaching and learning, mental and physical health), populations (e.g., students, teachers), and levels of education (e.g., school, higher education). To summarize the available literature on education during the pandemic both qualitatively and quantitatively, many systematic reviews and meta-analyses have begun to emerge. With the present systematic meta-review, we aimed to synthesize and combine this existing database to derive broader and more comprehensive insights that can aid educational stakeholders. We summarize and evaluate 43 systematic reviews, four meta-analyses, and eight combined systematic reviews and meta-analyses published until November 2022 to provide a comprehensive narrative of how this crisis affected education and what can be learned moving forward.

Keywords: COVID-19, corona, education, meta, review

Education around the world has faced unprecedented challenges as a result of the COVID-19 pandemic. While there have been many epidemics in human history, including the plague, bird flu, and the Spanish flu, the impact of the COVID-19 pandemic has emerged as being unique in terms of its vast disruptions to society and education. According to the United Nations (2020), it has drastically shaken the socioeconomic order of the world and impacted 63 million teachers and approximately 1.6 billion students at all educational levels in more than 190 nations across all continents. School children around the world have missed an estimated two trillion hours – and counting – of in-person instruction (United Nations Children's Fund et al., 2022). As such, the resulting loss of learning prospects for young people is expected to amount to substantial costs for the global economy in the long run (Psacharopoulos et al., 2021).

The first phase of reaction to the COVID-19 pandemic was characterized by global lockdowns, health concerns, and general uncertainty. Many countries experienced national closures that involved full shutdowns of educational institutions, ranging from preprimary schools to higher education institutions for extended periods of time. Classroom instruction was stopped, examinations were canceled or postponed, entrance exams and admission processes were delayed, universities were locked, and higher education students were asked to leave their dorms. The number of international students dropped drastically, and significant effects on the intellectual, emotional, and multicultural presence of education were observed (Tilak & Kumar, 2022).

Many believed that educational institutions would quickly reopen after being abruptly closed at the beginning of 2020. However, it soon became clear that schools and universities would not be reopening nor regular classes returning anytime soon, leading to a second response phase consisting of emergency remote teaching/learning. This instantaneous transition from on-campus to online learning was an *ad hoc* provision of online education that brought with it considerable changes in teaching and learning strategies for both teachers and students (Pelikan et al., 2021; Turnbull et al., 2021). Online teaching and learning characterized by digital tools, webinars, and online platforms became the new normal, leaving teachers and students with much to adjust to – especially given the abrupt transition and lack of information about when regular educational conditions would resume (Truzoli et al., 2021). Following these events as well as strict rules to control the spread of the virus and the eventual development and wide distribution of vaccines, education institutions cautiously started to reopen.

By the end of 2022, educational institutions in many countries resumed in-person operation and aspects of teaching and learning reverted to their prepandemic forms. Stimuli packages were coordinated, and educators began tackling the learning losses and costs brought forth by the pandemic. However, this remains a slow process. Education was not a priority in the COVID-19 stimulus packages offered by most governments (accounting for only 2.9% of the total; see UNESCO et al., 2020), and the COVID-19 pandemic has left a lasting impact on the educational sector – the effects of which will be visible for years to come. It has challenged educational systems with dramatic cuts to established practices and the imposition of new requirements. Consequently, the vast differences in how individual students, teachers, and parents, as well as different educational institutions and systems managed to cope with this unprecedented crisis are still being understood. By understanding and analyzing these differences, we can not only identify vulnerabilities in prepandemic educational practices and areas for growth but also use these insights to develop educational policies that can more effectively manage and mitigate future crises.

Given this background, considerable effort has been put forth by researchers across all stages of the pandemic to build a knowledge base of individual studies that can shed light on the impact of the COVID-19 pandemic on education. Indeed, the number of COVID-19-related research articles has skyrocketed since the beginning of 2020, with pandemic-related works having grown to represent a large proportion of all published articles (Brainard, 2022). According to the Web of Science database, more than 8,000 works have been published between 2020 and 2022 containing the keywords COVID and school, university, or education in their title alone. This surge of research was encouraged by many journals having waived their publication fees regarding COVID-19-related topics and expedited their publication processes (Palayew et al., 2020). While fast-paced delivery of research output was undoubtedly important to share new evidence in a timely manner, it may have also come at a cost in terms of quality (e.g., reduced objectivity, less rigorous peer review processes to support speed of knowledge dissemination, etc.). Aside from this, the sheer number of publications made it challenging to keep up with research on this topic (Brainard, 2022). As such, to draw conclusions from the vast amount of unique research works that have assessed COVID-19-related educational experiences and to subject them to quality control, many meta-analyses and systematic literature reviews have emerged. These reviews were conducted at different stages of the pandemic and, given the wealth of research on COVID-19 and education, often attended to rather specific and overlapping issues, necessitating a comprehensive overview.

We address this with the present work in the form of a systematic review that combines the information from existing meta-analyses and systematic reviews. Such a review is important in terms of bringing the separate findings together in a single place to be compared, thereby facilitating more extensive conclusions about the current research status of how education was impacted by COVID-19, as well as future directions.

The Present Systematic Review

We conducted a systematic meta-review of systematic reviews and meta-analyses that investigated the impact of COVID-19 on education. This includes findings of both individual and educational factors that operated as protective or risk factors for different populations (e.g., students, teachers) within different levels of education (e.g., primary school, higher education), as well as reviews more generally assessing teaching and learning, school closures, and interventions to support educational populations with the ramifications of the pandemic. As such, this meta study should provide a comprehensive overview to better understand how COVID-19 impacted education, expose gaps in current research, assess quality, and ultimately provide researchers, practitioners, and policy-makers with an overview of key outcomes and future directions.

Method

Literature Search and Eligibility Criteria

A search of systematic reviews and meta-analyses conducted between January 2020 and November 2022 was independently carried out by two co-authors using Scopus as well as the first 250 results from Google Scholar. Reference lists of the retrieved reviews were also scanned. We searched for reviews and meta-analyses that *systematically*[1] assessed COVID-19-related educational experiences in students and educators at primary, secondary, and tertiary levels. Our search term read as follows: "TITLE-ABS-KEY ((corona OR covid OR "cov-19" OR pandemic) AND (school* OR university OR college OR instructor OR pupils OR teacher OR teaching OR learner OR learning OR educat* OR undergraduate OR faculty) AND (meta-analysis OR review)) AND PUBYEAR AFT 2019".

Search filters were set to include peer-reviewed articles, book chapters, conference proceedings, and preprints published in English. Moreover, works were excluded if they were retracted or only review protocols, focused on a highly specific population (e.g., dentistry students in Austria) aside from those labeled as being at-risk (e.g., students with special educational needs), focused on a specific type of education (e.g., medical education, nursing education), or examined a mixed sample (e.g., the sample included a general population and did not explicitly investigate students or teachers).

Literature Screening Process

We used ASReview (van de Schoot et al., 2021), a machine learning application, to enhance our title and abstract screening during the literature screening process. In ASReview, the researcher interacts with an active learning model to screen abstracts. Starting with a preselection of training articles by the reviewers, the algorithm iteratively changes its relevancy predictions for the remaining abstracts based on the researcher's choices (relevant vs. irrelevant), thus aiding the selection process by grouping the records based on their relevance. Although it is possible to stop the screening process after a certain limit, we screened all abstracts to avoid false-negative decisions. Thus, ASReview was primarily used in the present study as a tool to reduce screening time. In comparison to a conventional screening method, this AI-assisted and open-source technology affords a more effective and error-free screening process (van de Schoot et al., 2021). We used the default Naïve Bayes classifier, term frequency-inverse document frequency (TF-IDF), and feature extraction and certainty-based sampling.

Quality Rating

To gauge the quality of the included reports, two raters coded each of the reports with regard to quality criteria based on the AMSTAR 2 instrument (Shea et al., 2017). We chose AMSTAR 2 because it is a widely used and confirmed instrument incorporating both systematic reviews and meta-analyses. Given that this instrument was originally developed with regard to healthcare interventions, we selected and slightly modified the items to align with the scope of the present investigation. As AMSTAR 2 is not intended to generate an overall score, we present the quality criteria for each item (good inter-rater reliability: κ = .84). To provide a full overview of the covered research, we considered all works, irrespective of their quality, but used the ratings to assess overall confidence in the results of the review when interpreting their findings.

Data Availability

We present a full table of the reviewed studies and summaries of their findings (Table 1) as well as an overview of the quality criteria of these reports (Table 2), a PRISMA flow diagram detailing the reports identified and included in our review (Figure 1), and the covered literature database as supplementary materials and in the Open Science Framework (OSF) at https://osf.io/9gudy/ (Daumiller et al., 2023).

Results and Discussion

Descriptive Information

As shown in Figure 1, our literature search identified 5,806 records. After the removal of duplicates and retracted articles, we screened the abstracts of 5,589 records and subsequently retrieved the full texts of 174 records. For two records, we were not able to retrieve a full text. After reading the full texts, a further 117 reports were excluded: Of these, 65 were not systematic reviews or meta-analyses, nine did not focus on COVID-19 and education, two were not in English, 38 pertained to a particular population or study program (e.g., dentistry students in Austria), and three addressed a general sample and not students or educators specifically.

Table 1 depicts an overview of all remaining 55 reports included in the systematic review. Most of them were systematic literature reviews (n = 43), followed by meta-analyses (n = 4) or combined systematic reviews and meta-analyses (n = 8). Using thematic synthesis (Thomas & Harden, 2008), we identified seven major themes that

---

[1] To operationalize *systematic*, we refer to the formulation of a research question and the identification of relevant individual studies (e.g., using specific search terms in literature databases), as well as the summarizing of those studies using explicit methodology (see Khan et al., 2003).

these works addressed. Through the same process, we highlighted relevant subfields, including recommendations for practice and future research. While partly overlapping, they placed a key focus on different aspects related to how COVID-19 affected education: well-being of students (n = 14), well-being of educators (n = 6), school closures and other school measures (n = 7), e-teaching and learning (n = 15), interventions (n = 3), individual factors (n = 5), as well as at-risk groups (n = 5). While most reports were clearly classifiable into one of these categories, some addressed multiple aims and were thereby independently grouped by two of the authors into the most relevant category based on the predominant topic of the paper. Only one discrepancy arose, which was resolved through discussion between the authors. In terms of scope and addressed works, some reports were quite similar; however, the majority were different from each other and contributed unique insights.

Table 2 provides an overview of the quality criteria of the reports. These ratings show that the quality of the works was mixed, with more than two thirds not fulfilling basic criteria, such as the provision of review questions, search strategy, and inclusion/exclusion criteria (which are also fundamental PRISMA criteria). Many also did not ensure sufficient reliability with regard to study inclusion and data extraction.

Next, we summarize the results and recommendations derived from the individual reports across the seven identified themes (for further details and specific references, see Table 1).

Well-Being of Students: Mental and Physical Health Problems

Students were uniquely affected by the COVID-19 pandemic due to drastic educational and lifestyle shifts related to physical isolation and the abrupt transition to virtual learning. Fourteen of the reviews retrieved from our literature search focused on examining mental health problems (n = 12) and physical health concerns (n = 2) in student populations.

Mental Health

Although the majority of the reviews (n = 10) focused on mental health in higher education students, some (n = 3) concentrated on mixed samples of school and higher education students, and only one review explicitly investigated school students. Regardless of school level, students reportedly faced a host of challenges during the pandemic, including reduction of face-to-face communication and physical activity (Deng et al., 2021; Xiang et al., 2020), disruption of social environments due to school and campus closures (Liyanage et al., 2022; Wang et al., 2022), as well as changes in career outlook and academic progress (Ebrahim et al., 2022; Zhu et al., 2021). These challenges carried the potential to exacerbate mental health problems, as elaborated below.

Prevalence of Mental Health Problems. Across the assessed reviews, the pooled prevalence estimates[2] of anxiety and depression in students ranged from 28% to 41% and 23% to 39%, respectively. Comparatively, a large-scale study assessing 13,984 college students' mental health across eight countries prior to the pandemic reported 12-month prevalence rates of anxiety and depression to be 16.7% and 18.5% (Auerbach et al., 2018). Moreover, the prevalence estimates of stress and fear symptoms of students during the pandemic were 31% and 33% (Fang et al., 2022). From a longitudinal perspective, Buizza and colleagues (2022) concluded that most studies in their review (12 of 17 studies) found an increase in anxiety symptoms, depression, mood disorders, or personality disorders when comparing students before and during the pandemic. Paralleling this, increases in distress, loneliness, alcohol use, as well as issues with externalization and attention were also observed.

Differences in Subgroups of Students. Several reviews found differential effects of the pandemic for certain groups of students. This included higher rates of anxiety in females compared to males, higher anxiety and depression in sexual and gender minorities compared to their nonminority counterparts (Buizza et al., 2022), higher mental health problems in students living in rural compared to urban areas (Elharake et al., 2022), as well as in the United States compared to Asian or European countries (Chang et al., 2021). Moreover, a higher prevalence of mental health problems was documented in students with financially poorer backgrounds and in those who lived alone compared to those who were financially stable and lived with others (Deng et al., 2021; Elharake et al., 2022; Jehi et al., 2022). Importantly, prevalence rates also differed depending on the assessment tools used and the country investigated (see Deng et al., 2021; Fang et al., 2022).

Physical Health

The pandemic additionally impacted students' physical health as a result of increased screen time, less physical activity, as well as unhealthy behaviors and sleep problems linked to psychological distress (Cortés-Albornoz et al.,

---

[2] Reported are the pooled estimates based on the prevalence rates of mental health problems reported in the individual studies assessed in the different systematic literature reviews and meta-analyses.

2022; Valenzuela et al., 2022). Specifically, Cortés-Albornoz and colleagues (2022) documented that most studies in their review (19 of 21 studies) found visual health in school students to worsen during the COVID-19 pandemic, while Valenzuela and colleagues (2022) found undergraduate students to have experienced sleep problems and, interestingly, also increased sleep duration. Regarding the latter point, the authors noted that increased sleep duration may not necessarily be beneficial, as it can negatively impact time spent on school work, social relationships, and mental health.

Summary of Recommendations and Future Directions
Several recommendations for supporting students' well-being throughout crises such as the COVID-19 pandemic were suggested throughout the reports. First, the offering of widespread access to mental health screenings and counseling services via internet and telephone was considered an important support measure. This was especially the case due to students not having been able to leave their residences and clinics being physically closed at certain phases of the pandemic. Within this, interventions centered around mindfulness, meditation, time management, relaxation, and physical exercise were often mentioned as promising methods for improving student health. Similarly, the promotion of healthy behaviors such as regular exercise, healthy diets, sufficient sleep, practicing social media hygiene, and avoiding alcohol or drug use were frequently suggested as ways to protect student well-being. As variations in findings depending on the assessed country were also evident, future research should acknowledge country differences when considering responses to the pandemic and associated student well-being.

Adding to this, teachers were also reported to have played important roles in student well-being through connecting students to appropriate mental health resources offered by educational institutions, creating stability in students' lives through well-structured courses, and offering accommodations in extenuating circumstances (see also Kiltz et al., 2020). Ensuring that students had timely access to accurate and easily understandable information about the COVID-19 pandemic in relation to their studies was considered essential for reducing fear and anxiety levels.

Well-Being of Educators: Less Studied but Similarly Affected
The pandemic also had an unprecedented impact on educators and their well-being. Considerably fewer reviews identified in our search focused on educators compared to students. Six reviews summarized the impact that pandemic-related changes had on different aspects of mental health in school and higher education teachers.

Mental Health
The rapid transition from established and familiar face-to-face teaching methods to online teaching threatened the well-being of school and higher education teachers (Daumiller et al., 2021). Specifically, this abrupt change came at a cost in terms of time and skill resources needed to convert learning materials to online contexts in a high-quality manner and was marked by confusion, poor work-life balance, lack of confidence and support, as well as concerns about students' academic progress and welfare (Ozamiz-Etxebarria et al., 2021; Susilaningsih et al., 2021; Zheng et al., 2022). In turn, high prevalence rates of mental health problems were observed in teachers during the pandemic, as elaborated on below.

Prevalence of Mental Health Problems. In the reviews identified in our search, the pooled prevalence of anxiety, depression, and stress among teachers during the pandemic ranged between 10%–49.4%, 16%–59.9%, and 12.6%–62.6%, respectively. Moreover, in their review containing longitudinal studies that compared experiences of teachers before and during the pandemic, Westphal and colleagues (2022) noted that some studies reported a decrease in feelings of accomplishment and an increase in depersonalization and emotional exhaustion.

Differences Between Subgroups of Teachers. Like with students, some groups of teachers appear to have struggled with their well-being more than others during the pandemic. This included teachers who were younger, female, had chronic health issues, and dealt with higher workloads (Ma et al., 2022; Silva et al., 2021). Moreover, while teachers in schools experienced higher prevalence rates of depression and anxiety, those in universities were comparatively less investigated but were also found to experience high levels of stress (Ozamiz-Etxebarria et al., 2021; Schwab et al., 2022).

Summary of Recommendations and Future Directions
Aside from teacher well-being being important in and of itself (Hascher & Waber, 2021), ensuring that teachers are feeling well and healthy is considered a critical step in fostering high-quality education for students. The most prominently reported suggestion aimed at supporting teachers' mental health in times of crises was to offer professional development opportunities geared at enabling teachers to optimally handle pandemic-related changes. Next, ensuring that teachers were provided with adequate materials and resources was considered a key factor (see e.g., Ozamiz-Etxebarria et al., 2021). This included the provision of sufficient IT support, technological software, and comfortable workspaces, as well as

up-to-date information and resources to best plan their teaching and accommodate their students. Lastly, the provision of mental health resources to help teachers deal with the emotional and psychological ramifications of the pandemic, including stress management strategies such as physical exercise and breathing techniques, were highlighted as protective factors for their well-being.

School Closures and Other School Measures: Intended and Unintended Effects

We found seven systematic literature reviews that engaged with school closures and other school measures. Most of this research focused on primary and secondary schools, while higher education institutions were less frequently examined.

Effects of School Closures

In terms of school closures, multiple problems were identified, including:

Restrictions of Students' Right to Education. A basic concern was that students' rights to education were restricted (Lorente et al., 2020). This issue is fundamental, as every human being has the right to a high-quality education (Robeyns, 2006).

Learning Losses. Despite the integration of remote learning, the results indicated learning losses similar to summer losses encountered by students with no teaching at all during the summer break ($d = -0.005$ SD to -0.05 SD per week; see Kuhfield & Tarasawa, 2020). These numbers are also mirrored by a recent meta-analysis reporting a pooled effect size of, $d = -0.14$ (Betthäuser et al., 2023), meaning that in total, students lost out on about 35% of a normal school year's learning. This shows that the majority of remote learning initiatives put in place during the first round of school closings in spring 2020 were not effective for student learning. However, findings also showed little evidence for an accumulation of learning deficits over time that was frequently feared (Betthäuser et al., 2023). In this context, few studies found that using online learning tools had a favorable impact on students' achievement. When favorable impacts were visible, this was mostly the case for students that were already familiar with working with online learning programs and did not have to adjust to a new learning environment.

Loss of Critical School-Based Services. Besides learning losses, problems were identified regarding critical school-based services becoming inaccessible due to school closures (e.g., healthcare, programs for children with disabilities, nutrition programs). This was particularly problematic in different low-middle-income countries where healthcare and nutrition was strongly embedded in school programs (Mayurasakorn et al., 2020).

Well-Being and Health. In addition to the disruption of daily routines, COVID-19 school closures were linked to mental and physical health concerns, particularly regarding negative emotional responses. These negative consequences became increasingly prominent the longer the lockdowns were in place. However, effects of school closures and larger societal lockdowns cannot be distinguished using data that are bound to the initial COVID-19 lockdown (Viner et al., 2022). The effects on well-being that were previously described are presumably the result of a variety of lockdown-related variables including social isolation, family stress, and general pandemic fears, as well as school closures. Nevertheless, there is compelling theoretical evidence that suggests school closures may have caused a significant fraction of these effects, especially harms to mental health by reducing social interactions with peers and teachers as well as limiting the role that schools play in supporting health-conscious behaviors among children and adolescents (Viner et al., 2022).

Increasing Social Inequalities. Alarmingly, school closures due to COVID-19 specifically impacted younger children and families with low socioeconomic status (see Hammerstein et al., 2021, regarding student achievement). Children with disabilities and those from lower-income families were especially affected by school closures during COVID-19 because they no longer had access to school-based resources and essential services needed to bridge socioeconomic gaps.

Other Measures

Besides physical closures of schools, additional measures were introduced which focused on enabling safer contact (e.g., mask wearing, hygiene, distancing, ventilation), reducing contact (reducing and alternating student numbers, reducing opportunities for contact), as well as surveillance and response (e.g., screening, testing, quarantine). However, these aspects were typically not comprehensively researched (Krishnaratne et al., 2020).

Summary of Recommendations and Future Directions

Looking forward, when considering closing schools in times of crises, the findings of the assessed reviews suggest that it is crucial to conduct tailored benefit and risk assessments specific to the socioeconomic environment, healthcare system, and educational resources in the area. Notably, most research conducted on school closures during the COVID-19 pandemic focused on developed countries. However, measures were implemented differently within different countries, further emphasizing the importance of considering the broader context that schools are situated in Tadesse and Muluye (2020). Adding to this, research should attend to potential unintended consequences of school closures (Kratzer et al., 2022), especially for students of low socioeconomic status. Therein, investigating additional health and social implications of school closures, such as the quality of life of children and their families, lifestyles, screen time, education/learning, cognitive development, as well as social connections (including social media use) was suggested as an important step forward. Beyond this, on a micro level, educational policy-makers should identify potential supportive measures that support time spent actively learning. On a larger scale, policy-makers should identify potential corrective actions to aid students in their learning, to prevent academic failure, and to build up mental health resources that are easily accessible for all.

E-Teaching and Learning: Opportunities, Challenges, and Psychological Impacts

Regarding e-teaching and learning, 14 systematic reviews and one meta-analysis were assessed. Most of these examined advantages and disadvantages of e-teaching during COVID-19. Some considered specific aspects such pedagogical implementations (Aisha & Ratra, 2022; Ibna Seraj et al., 2022), digital tools (Deepika et al., 2021), or students' attitudes, satisfaction, and learning outcomes (Masalimova et al., 2022; Nakhoda et al., 2021; Panagouli et al., 2021). Others engaged deeply with the roots of the problems that emerged and how they could be addressed (Na & Jung, 2021). All types of formalized educational levels (primary, secondary, and tertiary education) were considered, as well as the specific perspectives of students and teachers.

While a few studies sought to evaluate the merits of e-teaching and learning in general (e.g., Camilleri & Camilleri, 2022), most researchers were cautious about contrasting the digital education brought on by COVID-19 with regular digital education (Hodges et al., 2020). As opposed to well-planned online programs, this crisis-driven ad hoc *emergency remote teaching* was characterized, on the one hand, by a rapid transition frequently without adequate preparation for curricula, timetables, guidelines, technology infrastructure, content rights, etc., and on the other hand, by professional development for teachers and students to ensure successful teaching and learning (Bergdahl & Nouri, 2021).

With regard to advantages, disadvantages, psychological impacts, and recommendations for e-teaching and learning, these works addressed the impact of the change from face-to-face to virtual teaching on education, students' experiences and performance, the specific tools used to facilitate e-teaching, the respective policy-making, and the issue of equality (disparities between different social groups and its impact on accessibility and equity).

Opportunities

Multiple benefits and opportunities of e-teaching and learning were consistently identified in the covered works, extending beyond the emergency online teaching during COVID-19 (e.g., Aisha & Ratra, 2022; Deepika et al., 2021; Saikat et al., 2021). These include:

Accessibility. Through e-teaching, increased freedom and convenience for students to study and voice their ideas beyond time and geographical location were noted, along with wider access to education without discrimination. Especially during physical closures of secondary and tertiary institutions, e-learning was a sensible alternative for academic continuation.

Efficiency. Online programs were described as having the potential to be cost-effective, as they allow for saving on maintenance costs on physical campuses and reduce travel/commutes to and from colleges, meetings, conferences, and seminars. Regarding the latter point, the time cut down on commuting can be used more effectively for teaching and learning. Beyond this, online modes of education allow for learning material to be stored and updated more efficiently, and students can skip and repeat materials according to their own needs.

Individualization. It was acknowledged that e-learning can facilitate more individualized and thus effective learning, through self-regulation at one's own pace, higher autonomy, personalization, tracking of own progress, and opportunities for self-assessment.

Convenience. E-learning was noted as being more integratable with other aspects such as physical activity compared to traditional learning forms, thus also allowing for healthier lifestyles in general.

Resources. E-learning allowed access to more resources and opportunities to reuse them (e.g., rewatch videos) as well as a rich potential for interaction, discussion, and communication, also within large lectures.

Digital Literacy. Through exposure to technology itself, technological literacy gaps can be addressed, and expertise in online media fostered. This also allows for better preparation for technology-reliant job markets (however, the amount, duration, and difficulty must be adapted to the level of learners).

Further Skills. E-learning included innovative and additional methods to foster collaborative skills, self-regulation skills, problem-solving skills, etc.

Impetus for Change. The transition to e-learning exposed problems within the system and pushed educators to advance technological acceleration.

Challenges

Despite these opportunities, the quick transition to e-teaching and learning caught most teachers, institutions, and governments off guard (Fernández-Batanero et al.,

2022). The key challenges and disadvantages of e-teaching and learning that were identified in the reviews were as follows:

Communication. Due to lacking face-to-face contact, difficulties were noted with building, maintaining, and sustaining relationships; developing rapport; providing clear instructions; facilitating student engagement; and teaching with little feedback (especially when not seeing students' faces/reactions). Group work was also more complicated to facilitate, and increased external distractions and interruptions were noted. Also, on an organizational level, clearer strategies regarding communication and collaboration tools were called for.

Availability. Students often complained about teachers not being available. Teachers, in turn, complained about difficulties answering students' questions in real time and a lack of direct control over the learners in general.

Assessment. A key challenge was redesigning evaluations so that they fairly and reliably captured performance, especially in practical courses.

Misuse. Fraudulent acts by students (e.g., academic dishonesty) were observed, as well as concerns regarding data protection and breaches of privacy.

Workload. Increased workload, not only for teachers, but also for students, was also frequently mentioned.

Inadequacy. E-teaching was mostly not considered a complete substitute for traditional education because of its inherent limitations. This is especially true regarding learning requirements demanding hands-on instruction, practical work and fieldwork, live discussions, and/or specific laboratories, especially in numerical, experimental, medical, artistic, and communication fields.

Cost. Students and teachers struggled with acquiring adequate equipment and programs due to high prices.

Digital Literacy. Further support was noted as being necessary for teachers in their learning curve to be able to transition to hybrid and blended learning.

Technical Difficulties. Many technical difficulties emerged, including internet access and reception. Teachers faced numerous obstacles when trying to reach all students and when seeking to improve their work due to lacking resources.

Digital Divide. Especially nontech savvy teachers and students were unprepared and poorly equipped. Also for students without access to the necessary digital tools, e-learning was a large setback. Noted were large differences in the accessibility and quality of e-learning and teaching stemming from students' and institutions' economic backgrounds. As we will elaborate on later, this exacerbated differences between privileged and underprivileged students worldwide (Panagouli et al., 2021).

Psychological Impacts

Besides these insights into e-teaching and learning specifically, several issues were revealed that further compromised well-being of students and teachers above and beyond the issues already noted before the pandemic (Aisha & Ratra, 2022). Among these most frequently noted were as follows:

Worries. Worries, stress, doubts, and concerns about the e-learning curriculum were articulated. Anxiety was increased due to a lack of interpersonal communication. Students were particularly worried about potential academic loss and the changed instructional delivery.

Distress. Students and teachers were often already overwhelmed, and the transition to e-teaching was considered an additional stressor. Individuals frequently felt intimidated and reported low confidence due to online teaching and the delay in their study progress.

Work-Life Balance. Boundaries between academic and personal life ran the danger of becoming blurred, which was further increased when individuals were isolated at home.

Concentration and Motivation. Prolonged screen time affected concentration, and students reported a lack of motivation. Moreover, teachers reported feeling exhausted with regard to online teaching.

Summary of Recommendations and Future Directions

Taken together, the pandemic was considered a much-needed push for change in terms of digitalization. E-teaching and learning during the pandemic catalyzed innovations in education, proving the flexibility and convenience that teaching and learning online can provide. However, as observed during the pandemic, e-teaching and learning also comes with a series of challenges, and still more educational technology is available than can be applied for learning (Guppy et al., 2022). To reach its full potential of becoming as effective as face-to-face teaching (Francescato et al., 2006), future research is essential. Key suggestions to improve online teaching and learning experiences noted throughout the reviews include the following:

Policy-Making. The inequalities created through e-teaching need to be understood and mitigated, and accessibility and equity need to be ensured.

Training. Students and staff alike should be supported in terms of their motivation and digital literacy. Especially for rapid transitions, the difficulties and insecurities encountered by teachers regarding the implementation of such an educational mode need to be considered.

Tools. High-quality, accessible, user-friendly, error-free tools and platforms are required.

Diversity. A variety of learning resources should be provided to avoid monotony when learning online.

Feedback. Providing and receiving feedback needs to be ensured.

Student Centeredness. Effective e-learning environments should be centered around the individual students to meet their educational requirements.

Clarity. Instruction and expectations should be transparent and clear.

Psychological Impacts. E-teaching and learning bring a series of psychological impacts with them, especially under rapid transitions such as during the pandemic. This highlighted the necessity of taking care of the psychological well-being of students and teaching when learning online.

Blended and Hybrid Learning. Looking forward, a promising potential for enriching traditional learning formats lies in combining or switching between online and offline components, allowing students to interact with instructors, peers, and course material in both traditional classroom settings and online (Guppy et al., 2022).

Further Research. More research should be directed at examining the effectiveness of and the differences between traditional and online education to help teachers improve digital education techniques and development.

Interventions: Evidence on Specific Programs to Support Students

To support students in dealing with the ramifications of the COVID-19 pandemic, different interventions were developed to foster mental and physical health and in turn effective learning and adjustment. Specifically, three reviews identified in our search summarized the effectiveness of different types of online interventions used to promote health and mitigate anxiety and depressive symptoms among students. Notably, these interventions solely focused on higher education students; however, no reviews were identified which examined interventions aimed at supporting school students or teachers (who are characterized by substantially different learning needs).

Characteristics of Online Well-Being Interventions

Individual Versus Group Focus. While some interventions operated on an individual-level basis where students were asked to complete programs or materials independently with varied levels of support from trainers and psychologists, other interventions were group-based and entailed the provision of wider spread services to a larger number of students while promoting the exchange of experiences and building of support networks.

Platforms and Delivery Methods. In terms of virtual platforms used to host the different interventions, Zoom, Google Meet, Microsoft Teams, and Adobe Connect were reported as being frequently used. Regarding specific delivery methods, video conferencing, online chat tools, e-mails, discussion forums, and processing of asynchronous materials such as watching videos or reading information were most often mentioned.

Techniques. Regarding the different techniques used to promote well-being in students, mindfulness techniques (e.g., meditation interventions), cognitive behavioral therapies, dialectical behavior therapies, social support measures, online Isha Upa yoga, positive psychotherapy strategies, and breathing training programs were frequently reported.

Number of Sessions and Duration of Interventions. The number of sessions and duration of interventions varied substantially, with some interventions consisting of as little as one standalone session and others consisting of as many as 88 sessions across upwards of eight weeks.

Effectiveness

The majority of the online interventions were effective in promoting well-being of higher education students during the pandemic based on evidence from randomized clinical trials, quasiexperimental studies, and cohort or case-control studies (da Silva et al., 2022; Malinauskas & Malinauskiene, 2022; Riboldi et al., 2022). Within this, particularly online group mindfulness techniques and web-based cognitive behavioral therapies (da Silva et al., 2022), multicomponent online positive psychology interventions (Malinauskas & Malinauskiene, 2022), and individually catered cognitive behavioral therapies, dialectical behavior therapies, and mind-body practice techniques (Riboldi et al., 2022) emerged as being effective.

Summary of Recommendations and Future Directions

In terms of practice, the assessed reviews suggest that online interventions represent a promising way forward in supporting students both within and beyond crises such as the COVID-19 pandemic. Such interventions have the added benefit of being more cost-effective, easily accessible, and better positioned to cater to a wider and more geographically varied group. Research wise, interventions conducted during the pandemic should be examined more thoroughly to consider the effectiveness of specific strategies, stages of the pandemic in which such strategies were most effective (using longitudinal evidence), and relevant control variables.

Individual Factors: Risk Factors and Resources

Throughout the COVID-19 pandemic, students and educators differed in how they handled and experienced pandemic-related ramifications, where some fared better than others despite having seemingly similar external circumstances. To shed light on relevant factors that may have contributed to these differences, a total of five systematic reviews assessed different individual-level factors in students and educators and how they mattered for their experiences throughout the pandemic.

Motivation and Satisfaction. Students' motivation and satisfaction were considered important for their online learning experiences throughout the pandemic. Specifically, while their motivation levels mattered for their perceptions of and engagement in online learning, their satisfaction with education mattered for their well-being and subsequent online learning (Aznam et al., 2022). Learning structure, classroom interaction, facilities, and trainer knowledge were found to contribute to students' motivation and satisfaction.

Study Strategies. The study strategies that students employed throughout the pandemic also had an impact on their online learning experiences, where students' personal responsibility in learning activities, use of strategies, and self-regulated learning became increasingly important (Boström et al., 2021). Specifically, strategies used to avoid procrastination, set goals, self-monitor, self-instruct, and self-reinforce were particularly relevant. Moreover, the importance of the experience of authentic learning, as well as students' self-efficacy in how well they believed they could perform and handle the new online learning context were highlighted as important factors that mattered for their learning during the pandemic.

Social Media Use. Students' usage of social media during the pandemic had mixed effects on their mental health, including positive and negative effects, and in some cases, no statistically significant effects at all (Haddad et al., 2021). Following these mixed findings, it was suggested that a focus should be placed on preventing problematic social media use in students through moderation techniques rather than complete abstinence. This could be done by encouraging students to consciously assess their social media usage patterns in terms of how salient their use of social media is, whether they exhibit impulsive use of social media that negatively impacts their learning or whether they experience mood modifications and feelings of withdrawal from social media. Moreover, the establishment of media-free times, such as while eating meals or during studying, can be helpful. Importantly, social media was also considered to be an effective informational tool for quick and widespread access to information about the pandemic and surrounding regulations.

Personality Traits. Students' personality traits were also found to be associated with their learning experiences and well-being throughout the pandemic (see Morfaki & Skotis, 2022). Specifically, while agreeableness was linked to learning, it was also associated with perceived anxiety. Similarly, openness was associated with learning, self-efficacy, and satisfaction, yet also anxiety. Extraverted students reported lower course achievement and intrinsic motivational regulation as well as increased anxiety, presumably due to the online focus and loss of face-to-face learning opportunities. Finally, conscientiousness emerged as being beneficial and was consistently associated with academic achievement, self-efficacy beliefs, and effective learning styles.

Coping Mechanisms. Teachers often used coping strategies to deal with the ramifications of the pandemic. The most frequently used coping strategies that were considered beneficial for their mental health entailed reaching out for social support, physical exercise, taking part in leisure and spiritual activities, as well as reading and listening to music (Nang et al., 2022). Of these strategies, seeking social support was marked as the most popular strategy.

Summary of Recommendations and Future Directions

Looking forward, a focus should be placed not only on implementing broader strategies to support students and educators during crisis situations but also on the importance of considering individual differences and tailoring approaches to those who may particularly struggle. The reviews captured by our literature search indicate that *one-size-fits-all* approaches, although more feasible, may be shortsighted. Individuals' levels of motivation and satisfaction, study strategies, personality traits, and coping tendencies mattered for their experiences during the COVID-19 pandemic and should thereby be further acknowledged in future research and practical initiatives.

At-Risk Groups: Assessing and Closing the Gaps

As previously noted, the educational experiences of certain groups were more strongly affected by the COVID-19 pandemic than others. A total of five systematic reviews specifically addressed disadvantaged groups. A common finding across all reviews was that across most of the aforementioned outcomes, students from disadvantaged backgrounds were statistically significantly more and persistently negatively affected. This was due to a variety of obstacles, including long-term educational disengagement, digital exclusion, poor technology management, and increased psychosocial difficulties. Besides identifying at-risk groups, the respective studies also elucidated factors explaining why these groups were particularly affected and allowed for the formulation of takeaways of which gaps need to be closed and how, in future crises, such divides can be mitigated.

The specific at-risk groups identified included (1) individuals from poor and underdeveloped countries, (2) individuals with special educational needs and other disadvantages (e.g., hearing difficulties), (3) individuals from families with low socioeconomic status, particularly those who already had contact with social services, as well as (4) underprivileged students with subpar access to quality education, including those who started school behind or were already at the risk of disengagement.

Relevant Factors

Necessary Equipment and Technology. Especially for poorer and disadvantaged students, the availability of tools (such as computers to use for studying) was a prominent issue.

Accessibility and Usage of Learning Materials. Many students struggled due to limited access to learning materials (e.g., due to existence of appropriate materials or lacking internet connection). Parents of children with special needs reported that they spent considerable time and effort catering learning material to the individual needs of their children. Furthermore, availability does not guarantee quality online education for all groups. Instead, special training, quality measures, and additional features (e.g., captioning) may be required. Most importantly, this raises awareness of the need for educational systems to leverage teaching practices that can be easily implemented even amidst environmental crises and be more accessible during pandemic emergencies.

Routine Change. Especially for students with special educational needs (e.g., students with autism), routines were considered essential to lessen stress while encouraging a sense of order. Students' routines were disturbed when the lockdown started due to conflicting expectations and pressures from school, other agencies, and home working commitments. Many families struggled with changing existing and/or new routines and relieving pressure.

Partnerships and Collaboration. Crucial roles were performed by the interplay of authorities, educators, parents, and specialists in enhancing students' educational outcomes. Problems were frequently complex, and perspectives of everyone involved in education need to be included (García-Louis et al., 2022).

Special Needs. It was considered essential to offer special attention to those with special needs during such unprecedented changes (e.g., counseling and psychological services). Isolation left students feeling lonely and cut off from relationships with their peers, teachers, and the rest of their school community (Bakaniene et al., 2022). Inclusive education, however, aims to enhance a student's functioning and learning results by assisting them through the creation of supportive communities and by providing extra services, educational aids, or accommodations (Couper-Kenney & Riddell, 2021). Parents and parent–teacher collaboration and communication were noted as being important for their children's achievement. Thus, in crises, parents also need to be provided with the time and resources necessary to support their children, especially in terms of at-home learning.

Summary of Recommendations and Future Directions

Systemic imbalances, which have long hindered the academic progress of disadvantaged students, were clearly made worse by COVID-19. Often, the interconnection of a lack of resources, difficulties with mental health, and other aspects such as food hardship affected how students and their families responded to the pandemic. Given that it was mostly social inequities that already existed prior to the pandemic and severely limited the access of these at-risk groups to educational and employment opportunities, which in turn led to vast economic, food, and housing insecurity (García-Louis et al., 2022), it is critical that the aforementioned inequalities be acknowledged by institutional leaders and addressed at a national policy level (United Nations Children's Fund et al., 2022).

Limitations

Several limitations need to be considered when interpreting the findings of this systematic review. First, we only included topics that were relevant enough to have already been examined within multiple research works and in turn, within existing systematic literature reviews or meta-analyses. The inductive process of deriving categories based on existing studies provided us with insights into the directions in which research on the effects of COVID-19 on education is headed. Numerous systematic overviews existing are a strong indication of a topic's relevance. However, a more theory-based approach to preselecting (sub)topics may have provided different results. Second, although we brought together an immense amount of research findings, there is still a significant amount of primary research being reviewed on this topic at the time of publication. It also takes time to include already published work in systematic research syntheses. Although research syntheses focused on this specific time frame are necessary, the accelerated speed of publications during the pandemic and the urgency of robust findings may decrease their half-life/usefulness, which may in turn affect the implications proffered by this meta-review. Third, some reviews included forecasts as actual data of documented losses and based their conclusions primarily on this information (e.g., Zierer, 2021). Such practices are highly misleading, especially when seeking to inform the public debate on these topics. Finally, it is too early to evaluate the long-term effects of the pandemic on education, and it is important to be cautious when making predictions based on the available evidence collected thus far.

Implications

The quote "In the Middle of Difficulty Lies Opportunity" (attributed to John Archibald Wheeler) applies well to research practices and education alike in postpandemic times. What can we learn from the recent global crisis and which opportunities lie ahead?

As this will certainly not be the last crisis, the science community needs to be prepared and should consider changing their research practices. Robust, reliable, and trustworthy findings from different disciplines will be needed, ostensibly necessitating a trade-off between speed and rigor in doing research. More and higher-quality collaboration between researchers and disciplines as well as increased open science is needed to this end. Although many researchers already worked in a highly collaborative manner and shared data and preprints, joint and open research still needs to be intensified. This also pertains to the review articles we considered: A substantial number of reviews addressed the same topic and were published within the same year and journal, partly with subpar quality. These efforts would likely have been improved if researchers worked together right away and delivered fewer and higher-quality outputs. This should also aid in informing policy-makers and the public. In all phases of the pandemic, and also now, it has become evident that policy-makers *are* listening to researchers after all. Researchers pooling their efforts will therefore be an important asset in steering future crises.

In the midst of constant change, young people need a feeling of stability to digest, adapt, and develop new coping mechanisms. For many, education offers a great deal of stability. As we progressively recover from the pandemic, we must nurture the next generation to prepare them for the tragedies that will inevitably happen again but that we cannot predict. At the same time, COVID-19 increased the fission of our societies in many ways, including how unequally different groups were affected. These groups need to be more strongly considered to understand the effects of crises better (e.g., comparison of different groups sheds light on causal impacts) and to mitigate their effects (e.g., supporting those with lower human capital as a result of the pandemic, also through lifelong learning). Specifically, the impact of the pandemic on education has highlighted the socioeconomic setting in which only select groups may live and learn in safety. In addition, there was considerable variation in how different countries responded to the challenges of the pandemic and in turn the associated impact on the education systems, students, and teachers. More evidence is needed drawing on comparative research using equivalent approaches and measures. Thus, global efforts should be made to relaunch national and international education equity activities. Increased worldwide awareness of inequities might constitute a window of opportunity for programs promoting educational equity.

Moving forward, it is up to national educational policy-makers to be aware of these impacts and engage with the disciplines of educational and psychological research to put policies in place to lessen or even reverse adverse effects. This is arguably the most important societal responsibility for the post-COVID era to take on.

Conclusion

COVID-19 affected the educational sector on a global front. A vast amount of research was conducted within the (first) three years of the pandemic, illuminating the effects that the pandemic had on education. The pandemic also demonstrated the incredible ability of science to pivot amid a crisis. However, we still lack efficient methods for choosing, organizing, and presenting new findings in a way that maximizes comprehension and application. Even for experts in their respective (sub)fields, it was, and still is, difficult to remain up to date with the enormous number of papers being published on COVID-19. This is problematic, as urgent overviews are required in times of crises for science, policy, and practice. Even though overviews are available, the quality of these research syntheses is not universally adequate for transfer into policy (van de Schoot et al., 2021).

Therefore, in this paper, we provided an overview of systematic reviews and meta-analyses that investigated the impact of COVID-19 on education. In our systematic meta-review, seven major themes emerged that were addressed by previous syntheses: (1) the mental and physical health of students and (2) educators; (3) the role of school closures and other school measures; (4) e-teaching and learning and the opportunities, challenges, and impacts it brought with it; (5) interventions that were conducted to support students; (6) individual-level factors that made a difference; as well as (7) specific at-risk groups who particularly experienced disadvantages.

Specifically, the pandemic led to a time of anxiety and tense conversations about the existential crisis of humanity. Lockdowns, institutional closures, worries about continuing studies, and dim employment prospects all contributed to mental health problems in students. Early on in the pandemic, learning deficiencies quickly appeared and have not significantly narrowed since. Additionally, unexpected and ill-prepared distance learning, poor digital connectivity, subpar technology, and the inability of students to interact directly with peers and teachers strained students' mental and physical health, resulting in intense emotional anguish. In higher education, many students found the process of learning during COVID-19 to be so unpleasant that they ran the danger of losing interest in learning and deciding to drop out. Furthermore, it has also been difficult for teachers to work under such circumstances, and as a result, many have left the academic field and are looking for alternative employment to support themselves (Tilak & Kumar, 2022).

Moreover, as documented, an institution's and students' economic background significantly determined the quality of online learning and teaching, bringing along a new level of inequality among students worldwide (e.g., only 34% of students in Indonesia reported having a computer at home for academic work, compared to over 95% in Denmark, Slovenia, Norway, Poland, Lithuania, Iceland, Austria, Switzerland, and the Netherlands; OECD, 2020). Thus, the pandemic has revealed yet another ominous facet of educational disparity that transcends geographic and economic disparities (Tilak & Kumar, 2022).

References

Aisha, N., & Ratra, A. (2022). Online education amid COVID-19 pandemic and its opportunities, challenges and psychological impacts among students and teachers. *Asian Association of Open Universities Journal*, 17(3), 242–260. https://doi.org/10.1108/AAOUJ-03-2022-0028

Auerbach, R. P., Mortier, P., Bruffaerts, R., Alonso, J., Benjet, C., Cuijpers, P., Demyttenaere, K., Ebert, D. D., Green, J. G., & Hasking, P. (2018). WHO world mental health surveys international college student project. *Journal of Abnormal Psychology*, 127(7), 623–638. https://doi.org/10.1037/abn0000362

Aznam, N., Perdana, R., Jumadi, J., Nurcahyo, H., & Wiyatmo, Y. (2022). Motivation and satisfaction in online learning during COVID-19 pandemic. *International Journal of Evaluation and Research in Education*, 11(2), 753–762. https://doi.org/10.11591/ijere.v11i2.21961

Bakaniene, I., Dominiak-Świgoń, M., Meneses da Silva Santos, M. A., Pantazatos, D., Grammatikou, M., Montanari, M., Virgili, I., Galeoto, G., Flocco, P., Bernabei, L., & Prasauskiene, A. (2022). Challenges of online learning for children with special educational needs and disabilities during the COVID-19 pandemic: A scoping review. *Journal of Intellectual and Developmental Disability*, 48(2), 105–166. https://doi.org/10.3109/13668250.2022.2096956

Bergdahl, N., & Nouri, J. (2021). Covid-19 and crisis-prompted distance education in Sweden. *Technology, Knowledge and Learning*, 26(3), 443–459. https://doi.org/10.1007/s10758-020-09470-6

Betthäuser, B. A., Bach-Mortensen, A. M., & Engzell, P. (2023). A systematic review and meta-analysis of the evidence on learning during the COVID-19 pandemic. *Nature Human Behaviour*, 7(3), 375–385. https://doi.org/10.1038/s41562-022-01506-4

Boström, L., Collén, C., Damber, U., & Gidlund, U. (2021). A rapid transition from campus to emergent distant education. *Education Sciences*, 11(11), Article 721. https://doi.org/10.3390/educsci11110721

Brainard, J. (2022). 'COVID-ization' of research levels off. *Science*, 376(6595), 782–783. https://doi.org/10.1126/science.add0532

Buizza, C., Bazzoli, L., & Ghilardi, A. (2022). Changes in college students mental health and lifestyle during the COVID-19 pandemic. *Adolescent Research Review*, 7(4), 537–550. https://doi.org/10.1007/s40894-022-00192-7

Camilleri, M. A., & Camilleri, A. C. (2022). A cost-benefit analysis on the use of remote learning technologies: A systematic review and a synthesis of the literature. 6th International Conference on E-Education, E-Business and E-Technology, ICEBT 2022.

Chang, J. J., Ji, Y., Li, Y. H., Pan, H. F., & Su, P. Y. (2021). Prevalence of anxiety symptom and depressive symptom among college students during COVID-19 pandemic: A meta-analysis. *Journal of Affective Disorders*, 292, 242–254. https://doi.org/10.1016/j.jad.2021.05.109

Cortés-Albornoz, M. C., Ramírez-Guerrero, S., Rojas-Carabali, W., De-La-Torre, A., & Talero-Gutiérrez, C. (2022). Effects of remote learning during the COVID-19 lockdown on children's visual health. *BMJ Open*, 12(8), Article e062388. https://doi.org/10.1136/bmjopen-2022-062388

Couper-Kenney, F., & Riddell, S. (2021). The impact of COVID-19 on children with additional support needs and disabilities in Scotland. *European Journal of Special Needs Education*, 36(1), 20–34. https://doi.org/10.1080/08856257.2021.1872844

da Silva, G. C. L., Rossato, L., Correia-Zanini, M., & Scorsolini-Comin, F. (2022). Online group interventions for mental health promotion of college students. *Counselling and Psychotherapy Research*, 22(4), 844–852. https://doi.org/10.1002/capr.12561

Daumiller, M., Rinas, R., Hein, J., Janke, S., Dickhäuser, O., & Dresel, M. (2021). Shifting from face-to-face to online teaching during COVID-19: The role of university faculty achievement goals for attitudes towards this sudden change, and their relevance for burnout/engagement and student evaluations of teaching quality. *Computers in Human Behavior*, 118, Article 106677. https://doi.org/10.1016/j.chb.2020.106677

Daumiller, M., Rinas, R., Schoon, I., & Lüftenegger, M. (2023). Supplemental materials to "How did COVID-19 affect education and what can be learned moving forward? A systematic meta-review of systematic reviews and meta-analyses". https://osf.io/9gudy/

Deepika, V., Soundariya, K., Karthikeyan, K., & Kalaiselvan, G. (2021). Learning from home. *Postgraduate Medical Journal*, 97(1151), 590–597. https://doi.org/10.1136/postgradmedj-2020-137989

Deng, J., Zhou, F., Hou, W., Silver, Z., Wong, C. Y., Chang, O., Drakos, A., Zuo, Q. K., & Huang, E. (2021). The prevalence of depressive symptoms, anxiety symptoms and sleep disturbance in higher education students during the COVID-19 pandemic. *Psychiatry Research*, 301, Article 113863. https://doi.org/10.1016/j.psychres.2021.113863

Ebrahim, A. H., Dhahi, A., Husain, M. A., & Jahrami, H. (2022). The psychological well-being of university students amidst COVID-19 pandemic. *Sultan Qaboos University Medical Journal*, 22(2), 179–197. https://doi.org/10.18295/squmj.6.2021.081

Elharake, J. A., Akbar, F., Malik, A. A., Gilliam, W., & Omer, S. B. (2022). Mental health impact of COVID-19 among children and college students. *Child Psychiatry and Human Development*. https://doi.org/10.1007/s10578-021-01297-1

Fang, Y., Ji, B., Liu, Y., Zhang, J., Liu, Q., Ge, Y., Xie, Y., & Liu, C. (2022). The prevalence of psychological stress in student populations during the COVID-19 epidemic. *Scientific Reports*, *12*(1), Article 12118. https://doi.org/10.1038/s41598-022-16328-7

Fernández-Batanero, J. M., Montenegro-Rueda, M., Fernández-Cerero, J., & Tadeu, P. (2022). Online education in higher education. *Heliyon*, *8*(8), Article e10139. https://doi.org/10.1016/j.heliyon.2022.e10139

Francescato, D., Porcelli, R., Mebane, M., Cuddetta, M., Klobas, J., & Renzi, P. (2006). Evaluation of the efficacy of collaborative learning in face-to-face and computer-supported university contexts. *Computers in Human Behavior*, *22*(2), 163–176. https://doi.org/10.1016/j.chb.2005.03.001

García-Louis, C., Hernandez, M., & Aldana-Ramirez, M. (2022). Latinx community college students and the (in)opportunities brought by COVID-19 pandemic. *Journal of Latinos and Education*, *21*(3), 277–288. https://doi.org/10.1080/15348431.2022.2039152

Guppy, N., Verpoorten, D., Boud, D., Lin, L., Tai, J., & Bartolic, S. (2022). The post-COVID-19 future of digital learning in higher education. *British Journal of Educational Technology*, *53*(6), 1750–1765. https://doi.org/10.1111/bjet.13212

Haddad, J. M., Macenski, C., Mosier-Mills, A., Hibara, A., Kester, K., Schneider, M., Conrad, R. C., & Liu, C. H. (2021). The impact of social media on college mental health during the COVID-19 pandemic. *Current Psychiatry Reports*, *23*(11), Article 70. https://doi.org/10.1007/s11920-021-01288-y

Hammerstein, S., König, C., Dreisörner, T., & Frey, A. (2021). Effects of COVID-19-related school closures on student achievement. *Frontiers in Psychology*, *12*, Article 746289. https://doi.org/10.3389/fpsyg.2021.746289

Hascher, T., & Waber, J. (2021). Teacher well-being. *Educational Research Review*, *34*, Article 100411. https://doi.org/10.1016/j.edurev.2021.100411

Hodges, C. B., Moore, S., Lockee, B. B., Trust, T., & Bond, M. A. (2020). *The difference between emergency remote teaching and online learning*. http://hdl.handle.net/10919/104648

Ibna Seraj, P. M., Chakraborty, R., Mehdi, T., & Roshid, M. M. (2022). A systematic review on pedagogical trends and assessment practices during the COVID-19 pandemic. *Education Research International*, *2022*, Article 1534018. https://doi.org/10.1155/2022/1534018

Jehi, T., Khan, R., Dos Santos, H., & Majzoub, N. (2022). Effect of COVID-19 outbreak on anxiety among students of higher education. *Current Psychology*. https://doi.org/10.1007/s12144-021-02587-6

Khan, K. S., Kunz, R., Kleijnen, J., & Antes, G. (2003). Five steps to conducting a systematic review. *Journal of the Royal Society of Medicine*, *96*(3), 118–121. https://doi.org/10.1258/jrsm.96.3.118

Kiltz, L., Rinas, R., Daumiller, M., Fokkens-Bruinsma, M., & Jansen, E. P. (2020). When they struggle, I cannot sleep well either. *Frontiers in Psychology*, *11*, Article 2283. https://doi.org/10.3389/fpsyg.2020.578378

Kratzer, S., Pfadenhauer, L. M., Biallas, R. L., Featherstone, R., Klinger, C., Movsisyan, A., Rabe, J. E., Stadelmaier, J., Rehfuess, E., Wabnitz, K., & Verboom, B. (2022). Unintended consequences of measures implemented in the school setting to contain the COVID-19 pandemic. *Cochrane Database of Systematic Reviews*, *2022*(6), Article CD015397. https://doi.org/10.1002/14651858.CD015397

Krishnaratne, S., Pfadenhauer, L. M., Coenen, M., Geffert, K., Jung-Sievers, C., Klinger, C., Kratzer, S., Littlecott, H., Movsisyan, A., Rabe, J. E., Rehfuess, E., Sell, K., Strahwald, B., Stratil, J. M., Voss, S., Wabnitz, K., Burns, J., & Burns, J. (2020). Measures implemented in the school setting to contain the COVID-19 pandemic. *Cochrane Database of Systematic Reviews*, *2020*(12), Article CD013812. https://doi.org/10.1002/14651858.CD013812

Kuhfield, M., & Tarasawa, B. (2020). Projecting the potential impact of COVID-19 school closures on academic achievement. *Educational Researcher*, *49*(8), 549–565. https://doi.org/10.3102/0013189X20965918

Liyanage, S., Saqib, K., Khan, A. F., Thobani, T. R., Tang, W. C., Chiarot, C. B., Alshurman, B. A., & Butt, Z. A. (2022). Prevalence of anxiety in university students during the Covid-19 pandemic. *International Journal of Environmental Research and Public Health*, *19*(1), Article 62. https://doi.org/10.3390/ijerph19010062

Lorente, L. M. L., Arrabal, A. A., & Pulido-Montes, C. (2020). The right to education and ICT during COVID-19. *Sustainability*, *12*(21), Article 9091. https://doi.org/10.3390/su12219091

Ma, K., Liang, L., Chutiyami, M., Nicoll, S., Khaerudin, T., & Ha, X. V. (2022). COVID-19 pandemic-related anxiety, stress, and depression among teachers. *Work*, *73*(1), 3–27. https://doi.org/10.3233/WOR-220062

Malinauskas, R., & Malinauskiene, V. (2022). Meta-analysis of psychological interventions for reducing stress, anxiety, and depression among university students during the COVID-19 pandemic. *International Journal of Environmental Research and Public Health*, *19*(15), Article 9199. https://doi.org/10.3390/ijerph19159199

Masalimova, A. R., Khvatova, M. A., Chikileva, L. S., Zvyagintseva, E. P., Stepanova, V. V., & Melnik, M. V. (2022). Distance learning in higher education during Covid-19. *Frontiers in Education*, *7*, Article 822958. https://doi.org/10.3389/feduc.2022.822958

Mayurasakorn, K., Pinsawas, B., Mongkolsucharitkul, P., Sranacharoenpong, K., & Damapong, S. (2020). School closure, COVID-19 and lunch programme. *Journal of Paediatrics and Child Health*, *56*(7), 1013–1017. https://doi.org/10.1111/jpc.15018

Morfaki, C., & Skotis, A. (2022). Academic online learning experience during COVID-19—sa systematic literature review based on personality traits. *Higher Education, Skills and Work-based Learning*. https://doi.org/10.1108/HESWBL-03-2022-0062

Na, S., & Jung, H. (2021). Exploring university instructors' challenges in online teaching and design opportunities during the Covid-19 pandemic. *International Journal of Learning, Teaching and Educational Research*, *20*(9), 308–327. https://doi.org/10.26803/ijlter.20.9.18

Nakhoda, K., Ahmady, S., Fesharaki, M. G., & Azar, N. G. (2021). Covid-19 pandemic and e-learning satisfaction in medical and non-medical student. *Iranian Journal of Public Health*, *50*(12), 2509–2516. https://doi.org/10.18502/ijph.v50i12.7933

Nang, A. F. M., Maat, S. M., & Mahmud, M. S. (2022). Teacher technostress and coping mechanisms during COVID-19 pandemic. *Pegem Egitim ve Ogretim Dergisi*, *12*(2), 200–212. https://doi.org/10.47750/pegegog.12.02.20

Ozamiz-Etxebarria, N., Mondragon, N. I., Bueno-Notivol, J., Pérez-Moreno, M., & Santabárbara, J. (2021). Prevalence of anxiety, depression, and stress among teachers during the covid-19 pandemic. *Brain Sciences*, *11*(9), Article 1172. https://doi.org/10.3390/brainsci11091172

Palayew, A., Norgaard, O., Safreed-Harmon, K., Andersen, T. H., Rasmussen, L. N., & Lazarus, J. V. (2020). Pandemic publishing poses a new COVID-19 challenge. *Nature Human Behaviour*, *4*(7), 666–669. https://doi.org/10.1038/s41562-020-0911-0

Panagouli, E., Stavridou, A., Savvidi, C., Kourti, A., Psaltopoulou, T., Sergentanis, T. N., & Tsitsika, A. (2021). School performance among children and adolescents during covid-19 pandemic. *Children*, *8*(12), Article 1134. https://doi.org/10.3390/children8121134

Pelikan, E. R., Lüftenegger, M., Holzer, J., Korlat, S., Spiel, C., & Schober, B. (2021). Learning during COVID-19. *Zeitschrift für Erziehungswissenschaft*, *24*(2), 393–418. https://doi.org/10.1007/s11618-021-01002-x

Psacharopoulos, G., Collis, V., Patrinos, H. A., & Vegas, E. (2021). The COVID-19 cost of school closures in earnings and income across the world. *Comparative Education Review*, *65*(2), 271–287. https://doi.org/10.1086/713540

Riboldi, I., Cavaleri, D., Calabrese, A., Capogrosso, C. A., Piacenti, S., Bartoli, F., Crocamo, C., & Carrà, G. (2022). Digital mental health interventions for anxiety and depressive symptoms in university students during the COVID-19 pandemic. *Revista de Psiquiatria y Salud Mental*. https://doi.org/10.1016/j.rpsm.2022.04.005

Robeyns, I. (2006). Three models of education. *Theory and Research in Education*, 4(1), 69–84. https://doi.org/10.1177/1477878506060683

Saikat, S., Dhillon, J. S., Ahmad, W. F. W., & Jamaluddin, R. A. (2021). A systematic review of the benefits and challenges of mobile learning during the Covid-19 pandemic. *Education Sciences*, 11(9), Article 459. https://doi.org/10.3390/educsci11090459

Schwab, C., Frenzel, A. C., Daumiller, M., Dresel, M., Dickhäuser, O., Janke, S., & Marx, A. K. (2022). I'm tired of black boxes. *PLoS ONE*, 17(10), Article e0272738. https://doi.org/10.1371/journal.pone.0272738

Shea, B. J., Reeves, B. C., Wells, G., Thuku, M., Hamel, C., Moran, J., Moher, D., Tugwell, P., Welch, V., & Kristjansson, E. (2017). AMSTAR 2. *BMJ*, 358, Article j4008. https://doi.org/10.1136/bmj.j4008

Silva, D. F. O., Cobucci, R. N., Lima, S. C., & de Andrade, F. B. (2021). Prevalence of anxiety, depression, and stress among teachers during the COVID-19 pandemic. *Medicine (United States)*, 100(44), Article e27684. https://doi.org/10.1097/MD.0000000000027684

Susilaningsih, F. S., Komariah, M., Mediawati, A. S., & Lumbantobing, V. B. M. (2021). Quality of work-life among lecturers during online learning in COVID-19 pandemic period. *Malaysian Journal of Medicine and Health Sciences*, 17, 163–166

Tadesse, S., & Muluye, W. (2020). The impact of COVID-19 pandemic on education system in developing countries. *Open Journal of Social Sciences*, 8(10), 159–170. https://doi.org/10.4236/jss.2020.810011

Thomas, J., & Harden, A. (2008). Methods for the thematic synthesis of qualitative research in systematic reviews. *BMC Medical Research Methodology*, 8(1), 1–10. https://doi.org/10.1186/1471-2288-8-45

Tilak, J. B. G., & Kumar, A. G. (2022). Policy changes in global higher education. *Higher Education Policy*, 35(3), 610–628. https://doi.org/10.1057/s41307-022-00266-0

Truzoli, R., Pirola, V., & Conte, S. (2021). The impact of risk and protective factors on online teaching experience in high school Italian teachers during the COVID-19 pandemic. *Journal of Computer Assisted Learning*, 37(4), 940–952. https://doi.org/10.1111/jcal.12533

Turnbull, D., Chugh, R., & Luck, J. (2021). Transitioning to E-Learning during the COVID-19 pandemic. *Education and Information Technologies*, 26(5), 6401–6419. https://doi.org/10.1007/s10639-021-10633-w

UNESCO, UNICEF, & World Bank (2020). *What have we learnt?: Overview of findings from a Survey of Ministries of Education on National Responses to COVID-19*. https://policycommons.net/artifacts/1278937/what-have-we-learnt/1869007/

United Nations (2020). *Policy Brief: Education during COVID-19 and beyond*. https://unsdg.un.org/resources/policy-brief-impact-covid-19-children

United Nations Children's Fund, UNESCO, & World Bank (2022). *Where are we on education recovery?* UNICEF. https://eric.ed.gov/?id=ED619435

Valenzuela, R. L. G., Velasco, R. I. B., & Jorge, M. P. P. C., II. (2022). Impact of COVID-19 pandemic on sleep of undergraduate students. *Stress and Health*, 39(1), 4–34. https://doi.org/10.1002/smi.3171

van de Schoot, R., de Bruin, J., Schram, R., Zahedi, P., de Boer, J., Weijdema, F., Kramer, B., Huijts, M., Hoogerwerf, M., & Ferdinands, G. (2021). An open source machine learning framework for efficient and transparent systematic reviews. *Nature Machine Intelligence*, 3(2), 125–133. https://doi.org/10.1038/s42256-020-00287-7

Viner, R., Russell, S., Saulle, R., Croker, H., Stansfield, C., Packer, J., Nicholls, D., Goddings, A. L., Bonell, C., Hudson, L., Hope, S., Ward, J., Schwalbe, N., Morgan, A., & Minozzi, S. (2022). School closures during social lockdown and mental health, health behaviors, and well-being among children and adolescents during the first COVID-19 wave: A systematic review. *JAMA Pediatrics*, 176(4), 400–409. https://doi.org/10.1001/jamapediatrics.2021.5840

Wang, F., Zhang, L., Ding, L., Wang, L., & Deng, Y. (2022). Fear of COVID-19 among college students. *Frontiers in Public Health*, 10, Article846894. https://doi.org/10.3389/fpubh.2022.846894

Westphal, A., Kalinowski, E., Hoferichter, C. J., & Vock, M. (2022). K-12 teachers' stress and burnout during the COVID-19 pandemic. *Frontiers in Psychology*, 13, Article 920326. https://doi.org/10.3389/fpsyg.2022.920326

Xiang, M.-Q., Tan, X.-M., Sun, J., Yang, H.-Y., Zhao, X.-P., Liu, L., Hou, X.-H., & Hu, M. (2020). Relationship of physical activity with anxiety and depression symptoms in Chinese college students during the COVID-19 outbreak. *Frontiers in Psychology*, 11, Article 582436.

Zheng, M., Asif, M., Tufail, M. S., Naseer, S., Khokhar, S. G., Chen, X., & Naveed, R. T. (2022). COVID academic pandemic. *Frontiers in Psychology*, 13, Article 895371. https://doi.org/10.3389/fpsyg.2022.895371

Zhu, J., Racine, N., Xie, E. B., Park, J., Watt, J., Eirich, R., Dobson, K., & Madigan, S. (2021). Post-secondary student mental health during COVID-19. *Frontiers in Psychiatry*, 12, Article 777251. https://doi.org/10.3389/fpsyt.2021.777251

Zierer, K. (2021). Effects of pandemic-related school closures on pupils' performance and learning in selected countries. *Education Sciences*, 11(6), Article 252. https://doi.org/10.3390/educsci11060252

History
Received December 28, 2022
Revision received March 21, 2023
Accepted March 21, 2023
Published online July 18, 2023

Authorship
Martin Daumiller, conceptualization, methodology, software, investigation, formal analysis, visualization, writing – original draft, writing – review & editing; Raven Rinas, investigation, validation, writing – original draft, writing – review & editing; Ingrid Schoon, writing – review & editing; Marko Lüftenegger, conceptualization, methodology, writing – original draft, writing – review & editing. All authors approved the final version of the article.

Open Data
Supplementary materials as well as open data and materials are available in the OSF at https://osf.io/9gudy/ (Daumiller et al., 2023).

ORCID
Martin Daumiller
 https://orcid.org/0000-0003-0261-6143
Raven Rinas
 https://orcid.org/0000-0001-8907-0352
Ingrid Schoon
 https://orcid.org/0000-0002-4262-3711
Marko Lüftenegger
 https://orcid.org/0000-0001-8112-976X

Martin Daumiller
Department of Psychology
Universitätsstr. 10
86135 Augsburg
Germany
martin.daumiller@phil.uni-augsburg.de

Original Article

Comparison of Parent-Rated Teaching Activities During the First and Second School Lockdowns and Its Association With Students' Learning Outcomes During Distant Teaching

Ricarda Steinmayr[1], Rebecca Lazarides[2], Linda Wirthwein[1], and Hanna Christiansen[3]

[1]Department of Psychology, TU Dortmund University, Germany
[2]Department of Education, University of Potsdam, Germany
[3]Department of Clinical Child and Adolescent Psychology and Psychotherapy, Philipps University Marburg, Germany

Abstract: Due to the COVID-19 pandemic, schools were closed twice in Germany for several months. The aim of the present study was to investigate whether distant teaching activities increased from the first school lockdown to the second school lockdown and whether the frequency of distant teaching activities were related to students' outcomes (motivation, competent and independent learning, perceived learning progress) during distant learning. To this end, $N = 3{,}480$ legal guardians filled in an online questionnaire during the second lockdown (see Steinmayr et al., 2021). Distant teaching activities greatly increased from the first lockdown to the second lockdown. Besides communication with a parent, all other distant teaching activities were more frequent at secondary schools. However, in both elementary and secondary schools, distant teaching activities varied greatly. Distant teaching activities as well as children's characteristics and social background were independently important for students' outcomes. The results are discussed with regard to their practical implications for realizing distant teaching.

Keywords: COVID-19, distant teaching, teaching quality, motivation, perceived competencies

The two school lockdowns in Germany due to COVID-19 in 2020 and 2021 faced students, parents, and teachers with new challenges. During the first lockdown in Germany, the prerequisites for distant teaching were not given at most schools (e.g., König et al., 2020), which resulted in an undesirable realization of distant teaching (Steinmayr et al., 2021). Before the second lockdown in Germany (December 2020), the government had time and financial investments to prepare schools better (May & Hoerl, 2022). In both lockdowns, the Ministries of Education of all federal states completely allocated the realization of distant teaching to the schools (see also Fickermann & Edelstein, 2020). Thus, the quality of distance teaching greatly varied between schools in the first lockdown (see Steinmayr et al., 2021). As teaching quality is an important prerequisite for students' academic achievement, motivation, and emotion (e.g., Lazarides & Buchholz, 2019), the teaching activities during the first school lockdown and their respective quality (in the following labeled as distant teaching activities) were related to students' motivation, learning behaviors, and academic achievement (Steinmayr et al., 2021). The aim of this study thus is to compare the frequency of teaching activities during the first and second school lockdowns and to replicate the results by Steinmayr and colleagues.

Effects of Infection Control Interventions on Children and Adolescents

Overall, the pandemic-caused school closures and disruption of family routines had massive consequences on the children worldwide (for a review, see Panchal et al., 2021). The results of the German COPSY study, which surveyed students between 12 and 17 years, showed that school closures were associated with an increase in mental health impairment and the perception that the school situation is burdensome, whereas the school openings in the fall of 2021 were associated with improvements in those factors

(Ravens-Sieberer et al., 2022). In a longitudinal study, Steinmayr and colleagues (2022) demonstrated a decline in affective subjective well-being by testing an elementary school sample before and during the pandemic.

As teachers were unprepared when schools closed the first time and digital equipment was insufficient at German schools (Lorenz et al., 2020), the government invested a lot of money to equip teachers with digital teaching and communication devices. In the end, most teachers had a laptop or tablet by which they were able to realize distant teaching. However, having the means to teach in distance does not equal that distant teaching is realized on a frequent basis. Thus, one aim of the present study was to check whether the realization of distant teaching changed from the first lockdown to the second lockdown.

Distant Teaching Activities During the COVID-19 Pandemic

Students' motivational and cognitive development in learning settings is shaped by the teaching practices they experience in class (Pianta & Hamre, 2009). The Three Dimensions of Teaching Quality framework of Klieme and colleagues (2009) describes three basic dimensions of effective teaching. *An effective classroom management* is defined, for example, by actions of the teacher to establish order or to elicit cooperation among students. *Cognitive activation* refers, for example, to the encouragement of students to develop their own solutions, to try out multiple solution paths, and to critically evaluate their own solutions. *Learning support* is particularly important for students' motivational development and is characterized, for example, by emotional supportive teacher–student relationships and adaptive learning support. Against this background, research has emphasized that distant teaching during the COVID-19-related school lockdown also needs to consider the implementation of teaching quality (Voss & Wittwer, 2020). As the recently published meta-analysis by Betthäuser and colleagues (2023) has shown, studies on distance education during the school closures display generally negative effects on students' learning outcomes, especially when belonging to marginalized groups (see also Darling-Aduana et al., 2022). Huber and Helm (2020) report that the feedback that students reported to have received from their teachers was positively associated with their self-reported learning success and with time spent with learning activities. The student-reported quality of the contact between students and their teachers during the school closures was negatively associated with learning success but positively associated with students' positive emotions and time spent with learning activities. The level of self-reported self-directed learning was positively associated with positive emotions, learning activities, and learning success. Similarly, Steinmayr and colleagues (2021) showed that distant teaching activities that involve direct forms of interpersonal feedback and communication particularly contributed to elementary and secondary school students' academic outcomes during school lockdown. Furthermore, more recent findings showed that instructional quality during distance education contributed little to explaining students' learning effort and intrinsic motivation (Helm & Huber, 2022).

Student and Family Characteristics

Family and students' characteristics are important for students' motivation (e.g., Steinmayr et al., 2012). Therefore, students' achievement motivation and their academic achievement during homeschooling should be substantially related to students' abilities, personality/temperament, and school engagement. In line with Steinmayr and colleagues (2021), we included the following student characteristics as possible confounding factors in our study: parents' perceptions of students' abilities in the domains of math and German, students' negative emotionality (as a facet of their personality/temperament), and students' school engagement. We chose school engagement as well as math and language art competencies as they had the highest relative importance for school achievement in previous studies (e.g., Steinmayr et al., 2018). As homeschooling requires a lot of emotional self-control, we also assessed negative emotionality. The findings demonstrated substantial relations between these factors and students' motivation and achievement in elementary and secondary schools (e.g., Steinmayr et al., 2018, 2021). This was also true for students' motivation, independent and competent learning, and perceived learning progress during the first lockdown (Steinmayr et al., 2021). The findings also demonstrated the association between social background variables and academic achievement as well as learning motivation during the pandemic (e.g., Heyder et al., 2020). Furthermore, learning losses were especially pronounced for socially disadvantaged students (Ludewig et al., 2022). Thus, we also included variables assessing students' socioeconomic background, e.g., parents' highest school leaving certificate. Moreover, we asked for the child's and parent's age, migration background, and gender. Gender was related to both students' learning outcomes during the first lockdown (Steinmayr et al., 2021) and a decrease in academic achievement after the first lockdown (Breaux et al., 2021).

Aims of the Present Study

Only few studies investigated distant teaching realization in the second lockdown (e.g., Alves et al., 2022; Wößmann et al., 2021). We are not aware of a study that systematically compared the first and second school lockdowns concerning the realization of distant teaching in different subjects in elementary and secondary schools.

Therefore, the first aim of the present study was to investigate how distant teaching was realized in different subjects during the second school lockdown in schools in Germany. In line with Steinmayr and colleagues (2021), we expected that different forms of distant teaching (e.g., grading, sending tasks vs. task-related feedback, provision of solutions, direct communication with students and parents) would differ across school types and would be differentially associated with students' motivation, learning behaviors, and achievement during the school lockdown. Furthermore, studies indicated that students' individual characteristics and family-related socioeconomic resources were substantially associated with students' motivation, their behavior, and achievement during the school lockdown (e.g., Huber & Helm, 2020; Sliwka & Klopsch, 2020).

Against this background, we investigated the following hypotheses:

Hypothesis 1: The frequency of distant teaching activities differs between elementary and secondary schools.

Hypothesis 2: The frequency of distant teaching activities differs between the first and second lockdowns for both elementary and secondary schools.

Hypothesis 3: The frequency of distant teaching activities is positively associated with students' motivation, competent and independent learning, and learning progress during the school lockdown.

Hypothesis 4: Distant teaching activities that involve direct forms of interpersonal feedback and communication (e.g., task-related feedback, teaching via videoconference, and student–teacher communication) are particularly strongly related to students' motivation, competent and independent learning, and learning progress during the school lockdown when simultaneously considering other forms of distant teaching activities (e.g., grading, frequency of sending out tasks).

Hypothesis 5: Students' characteristics and social background variables add to the variance explanation of students' motivation, competent and independent learning, and learning progress during the school lockdown above distant teaching activities.

Method

Procedure

The study was conducted online. Parents filled in the online questionnaire between January and March 2021 during the second school lockdown in Germany of the global *Corona crisis* (the COVID-19 pandemic). To reduce the risk of infection, most schools had been closed in Germany from before Christmas 2020 onward for several weeks, for most grades at least until Easter holidays 2021 and beyond. We recruited parents from all over Germany by posting the study link on Facebook.com, Twitter.com, and other social networks (e.g., Bing). Additionally, we contacted 28 parent associations from all federal states in Germany in January 2021 by e-mail. Finally, we disseminated the study link by ourselves via our university homepages and via personal contacts and e-mail distribution lists.

The online questionnaire was nearly identical to the one used by Steinmayr and colleagues (2021). The completion of the online questionnaire took the parents about 20 min. If they had more than one child in the school, parents were asked to indicate for which child they filled in the questionnaire.

Participants

A total of 3,480 adults from all German federal states were included in the study. The mean age of the parents was 43.34 years (SD = 5.71). The majority of parents were female (n = 3,040; male: n = 437; other: n = 3), were born in Germany (n = 3,230), and had some kind of university entrance certificate [(Fach-)Abitur] (n = 2,557). Of all participating subjects, n = 3,076 indicated to be the mother of the child for whom they filled in the questionnaire (father: n = 375; different responsible relationship to the child: n = 29). The sample was representative for the German population with respect to mean age (Federal Statistical Office, 2020b). However, females and parents with a university entrance certificate were overrepresented in the sample (Federal Statistical Office, 2020a, 2020b).

The mean age of the rated children was 10.97 (SD = 2.96), of whom n = 1,696 were female (male: n = 1765; other: n = 19). Children attended the following school types: elementary school: n = 1,373; academic track secondary schools (Gymnasium): n = 1,378; comprehensive secondary schools (Gesamtschule): n = 375; intermediate track secondary schools (Realschule): n = 264; lowest track secondary schools (Hauptschule): n = 29; schools for special educational needs (Förderschule): n = 23; and other school type: n = 38. Children were in Grades 1–13.

At the time their parents participated in this study, children had to learn at home because of the school lockdown for 7.59 weeks on average (SD = 3.97 weeks). We excluded parents of children who attended a school for special educational needs because these children have systematically different needs than students who are attending regular schools. Furthermore, we excluded parents whose children attended a different school type than the Gymnasium, Gesamtschule, Realschule, and Hauptschule. The final analysis sample of this study thus comprised 3,419 participants, of whom n = 1,373 attended an elementary school and n = 2,046 attended a secondary school. This distribution of elementary (40%) and secondary school students (60%) was similar to the distribution in the population of German students in 2020/2021 (elementary: 36%; secondary: 64%). A MANOVA with both gender and age variables as well as the indicator of sociodemographic background demonstrated that the present sample slightly differed from the sample in the first lockdown (see Steinmayr et al., 2021). Subsequent ANOVAs showed that the case was statistically significant ($p < .05$) for having an own room ($F = 12.74$), highest school leaving certificate ($F = 18.52$), child's age ($F = 5.42$), and both gender variables (parent: $F = 14.37$; child: $F = 15.67$). However, all effect sizes were $\eta^2 < .003$. Thus, samples assessed in the first and second lockdowns were nearly identical.

Instruments

All scales used in the present paper had been identically assessed and described in detail in Steinmayr and colleagues (2021). Reliabilities for all measures are reported in the Electronic Supplementary Material (ESM 1), Supplement 1, and are high.

Motivation During the School Lockdown. Students' motivation was assessed with the following items: "My child works motivated on the assignments during the school lockdown" and "My child enjoys working on her/his assignments during the school lockdown." Parents were asked to read through the items and indicate whether the following statements apply to their situation at home during the school lockdown. They answered the items on a 5-point Likert scale ranging from 1 (*strongly disagree*) to 5 (*strongly agree*). The two items were combined to a motivation during the school lockdown scale.

Competent and Independent Learning During the School Lockdown. The items were the following: "My child accomplishes her/his assignment during the school lockdown without any difficulties," "My child only accomplishes her/his assignment during the school lockdown with my or my partner's help" (reversely coded), and "My child needs a lot of support for doing her/his school tasks during the school lockdown" (reversely coded). Parents answered the items on the same scale as the motivation items.

Learning Progress During the School Lockdown. The item "My child learns a lot during the school lockdown" assessed parents' perception of their child's learning progress during the school lockdown. Parents answered the item on the same scale as the motivation items. The item correlated in the expected direction with the other items; for example, correlation with motivation during the school lockdown was high.

Distant Teaching Activities. Eight different distant teaching activities were assessed via eight items assessing the perceived frequency at which different teachers realized these aspects. According to Steinmayr and colleagues (2021), we focused on mathematics, language arts, English, and science (elementary school) and biology teachers (secondary school). Specifically, we asked parents for the frequency at which the respective teacher sent tasks and solutions, requested students' solutions, gave feedback on those, graded students' solutions, taught via videoconference, and had contact with the child and/or parent via chat, e-mail, or phone. Answers were given on a scale with six answer options: 1 (*not yet*), 2 (*every 3 weeks*), 3 (*every 2 weeks*), 4 (*every week*), 5 (*twice per week*), and 6 (*three times per week or more*). Parents were asked to answer these questions for every subject even if the same teacher taught these subjects. Items referring to the same distant teaching activity were summed up indicating how this aspect of distant teaching was realized in general at the school that the rated child attended. Reliabilities were at least satisfactory. We additionally asked parents whether distant teaching was organized via videoconferences according to their child's regular timetable (with the exception of sports). Answering options were *no*, *yes*, and *other*. The item was dummy-coded with *no* and *other* = 0 and *yes* = 1.

Parent Ratings of Student Characteristics. Parents were instructed to compare their child with children of the same age when rating their child's negative emotionality, school engagement, and math and language arts abilities in general. Parents answered all items on a 7-point scale. All items had previously been used in a parent survey (see Steinmayr et al., 2021).

Negative Emotionality. Parents' perception of their child's negative emotionality was assessed with the following four items which were adapted from the *Personality questionnaire for children between the ages of 9 and 14* (Persönlichkeitsfragebogen für Kinder zwischen 9 und 14 Jahren/PFK 9–14; Seitz & Rausche, 2019): "My child is easily annoyed about something," "It is mostly difficult for my child to be patient," and "My child gets angry quickly."

School Engagement. We used the short version of the Behavioral Engagement and Disaffection scales developed by Skinner and colleagues (2008). We assessed behavioral engagement with the following items: "My child tries hard to do well in school," "My child listens carefully if someone explains something to her/him," and "My child always takes an effort to do her/his homework well."

Math and Language Arts Abilities. Parents' perception of their child's abilities in the domain of math was assessed by the following three items (adapted from Lorenz, 2011): "My child is talented in math," "My child has a good understanding of mathematical relations," and "My child can solve arithmetic problems well." Parents' perception of their child's ability in the domain of language arts was assessed by the following four items (adapted from Lorenz, 2011): "My child is talented in German," "My child can understand texts well," "My child has an extensive vocabulary," and "My child can read well."

Social Background. Four items assessed families' social background. First, we asked for the rater's highest school leaving certificate. The variable was dummy-coded by recoding no or vocational track leaving certificates as 0 and both academic track school leaving certificates as 1. *Others* were coded as missing. Second, parents indicated if they were born in Germany or in a different country as a measure of migration background. The variable was also dummy-coded with 0 (*born in Germany*) and 1 (*not born in Germany*). Third, we assessed whether the rated child had a bedroom for them and whether the child had a computer or tablet at their disposal for their assignments during the school lockdown (see Wendt et al., 2017). Answer options for the latter two items were 0 (*no*) and 1 (*yes*).

Further Demographics. Additionally, we considered children's and parents' age and gender. Gender was dummy-coded with 0 (*male*) and 1 (*female*).

Statistical Analyses

Descriptive statistics and multivariate analyses of variance were calculated with SPSS 28. When conducting MANOVAs to test Hypotheses 1 and 2, we first ran them with demographic variables as covariates as the samples in the first and second lockdowns slightly differ. However, as none of the demographic variables reached statistical significance, the results are presented without covariates. We used Mplus version 7.4 (Muthén & Muthén, 1998–2015) for all other analyses using the same analytical approach as in Steinmayr et al (2021). We accounted for missing data by applying full information maximum likelihood estimation (Enders & Bandalos, 2001). For the structural equation models (SEM), we refer to the comparative fit index (CFI), the root mean square error of approximation (RMSEA) along with its associated CIs, the standardized root mean squared residual (SRMR), and the chi-square test statistic to evaluate goodness of fit of the tested models (Goodboy & Kline, 2017). The SEMs were set up in the following way: In the first model, parent-rated student's motivation, competent and independent learning, and learning progress during distant learning were simultaneously regressed on the eight distant teaching activities. Perceived motivation and competent and independent learning were modelled as latent factors and learning progress as a manifest variable. Then, parent-rated student's motivation, competent and independent learning, and learning progress were additionally regressed on parent-rated child's general negative emotionality, school engagement, abilities in math and language arts (all modelled as latent factors), dummy-coded parent's highest school leaving certificate, migration background, possession of a laptop or a tablet during school lockdown, possession of an own bedroom, and child's and parent's gender and age (for more details, see ESM 1, Supplement 2). Analyses were run separately for elementary and secondary schools. We checked whether secondary schools differed in the models described below. We found no statistically or practically significant differences. Thus, we decided to perform all analyses for the combined secondary school sample.

Results

Descriptive Statistics and Frequencies

Table 1 displays the results MANOVAs yielded concerning difference in distant teaching activities between measurement points (first and second lockdowns) and elementary and secondary schools. The data used for the first lockdown had already been published in Steinmayr and colleagues (2021). Frequencies of distant teaching activities for the second lockdown are reported in ESM 1, Supplement 3.

The results demonstrated, in line with Hypothesis 1, that the frequency of teaching activities differed between elementary and secondary schools (between different secondary school types, they did not differ statistically significant). Besides *communication with a legal guardian*, all teaching activities were more frequent in secondary schools (see ESM 1, Supplement 3, Table E2). MANOVAs yielded effect sizes ranging between $\eta^2 = .03$ (grading) and $\eta^2 = .35$ (sending tasks). Furthermore, in line with Hypothesis 2, distant teaching activities greatly increased from the first school lockdown to the second school lockdown in both school levels (see also ESM 1, Supplement 4). MANOVAs yielded especially large effect sizes for the frequency by which teacher taught via videoconferences ($\eta^2 = .33$). However, variances for all distant teaching activities were still huge in both school levels.

Table 1. Multivariate analyses of variance with mean frequencies of different distant teaching activities as the dependent variables and type of school (elementary vs. secondary school) and time of measurement (first vs. second lockdown) as independent variables and subsequent univariate analyses of variance

Teaching activities	1. Lockdown M ES	1. Lockdown M SecS	1. Lockdown SD ES	1. Lockdown SD SecS	2. Lockdown M ES	2. Lockdown M SecS	2. Lockdown SD ES	2. Lockdown SD SecS	ANOVAs Lockdown F	ANOVAs Lockdown η^2	ANOVAs School F	ANOVAs School η^2	ANOVAs Lockdown × school F	ANOVAs Lockdown × school η^2
How often did the following teacher…														
… sent tasks?									**281.62**	**.19**	**654.93**	**.35**	**44.96**	**.04**
Math teacher	3.68	4.00	0.90	0.89	4.15	4.78	0.82	0.92	690.91	.11	398.09	.06	44.99	.01
Language arts teacher	3.68	3.92	0.91	0.90	4.15	4.69	0.80	0.94	666.82	.10	271.54	.04	36.93	.01
English teacher	2.12	3.96	1.35	0.88	3.26	4.67	1.32	0.93	907.92	.14	2,770.04	.34	47.23	.01
Biology/science teacher	2.46	3.29	1.39	1.18	3.58	4.03	1.18	0.88	825.10	.14	385.18	.07	33.77	.01
… sent solutions?									**89.57**	**.07**	**337.22**	**.22**	**3.74**	**<.01**
Math teacher	2.38	3.41	1.59	1.34	2.96	4.05	1.78	1.44	217.01	.04	661.53	.10	*0.39*	
Language arts teacher	2.31	2.92	1.55	1.53	2.91	3.67	1.78	1.67	235.40	.04	239.24	.04	*2.97*	
English teacher	1.59	3.12	1.19	1.48	2.38	3.77	1.63	1.58	288.65	.05	1,183.02	.18	*2.75*	
Biology/science teacher	1.76	2.53	1.32	1.46	2.53	3.29	1.68	1.47	332.34	.06	332.30	.06	*0.01*	
… requested students' solutions?									**313.32**	**.21**	**374.93**	**.24**	**2.93**	**<.01**
Math teacher	2.40	3.27	1.52	1.45	3.73	4.39	1.44	1.24	1,062.82	.16	408.30	.07	8.20	<.01
Language arts teacher	2.49	3.20	1.50	1.41	3.75	4.35	1.41	1.18	1,077.29	.16	315.59	.05	*2.07*	
English teacher	1.63	3.22	1.21	1.41	2.91	4.34	1.63	1.18	981.54	.16	1,555.39	.23	4.73	<.01
Biology/science teacher	1.83	2.68	1.29	1.44	3.14	3.76	1.55	1.13	974.29	.16	368.85	.07	8.70	<.01
… gave feedback on students' solutions?									**226.81**	**.16**	**155.19**	**.12**	**7.99**	**<.01**
Math teacher	2.01	2.41	1.40	1.51	3.44	3.39	1.57	1.66	807.19	.13	17.71	<.01	28.11	<.01
Language arts teacher	2.11	2.40	1.43	1.48	3.53	3.34	1.54	1.61	802.25	.13	*1.30*		34.59	<.01
English teacher	1.42	2.44	1.02	1.49	2.61	3.39	1.65	1.63	613.93	.11	436.13	.08	8.58	<.01
Biology/science teacher	1.57	1.97	1.14	1.35	2.91	2.86	1.62	1.50	750.56	.13	18.40	<.01	28.51	<.01
… graded students' solutions?									**57.38**	**.05**	**34.97**	**.03**	**9.73**	**<.01**
Math teacher	1.15	1.19	0.61	0.71	1.46	1.70	1.12	1.29	220.63	.04	23.92	<.01	12.70	<.01
Language arts teacher	1.16	1.20	0.61	0.72	1.47	1.70	1.12	1.26	214.92	.04	23.64	<.01	11.90	<.01
English teacher	1.08	1.20	0.46	0.73	1.29	1.72	0.89	1.27	175.31	.03	98.64	.02	31.07	<.01
Biology/science teacher	1.09	1.14	0.47	0.59	1.38	1.58	1.00	1.11	220.27	.04	27.23	<.01	10.00	<.01
… taught via videoconference?									**572.08**	**.33**	**192.01**	**.14**	**58.49**	**.05**
Math teacher	1.28	1.80	0.89	1.35	3.05	3.87	2.00	1.70	1963.46	.26	239.18	.04	12.24	<.01
Language arts teacher	1.32	1.67	0.93	1.28	3.19	3.81	2.01	1.71	2,153.55	.28	129.27	.02	9.66	<.01
English teacher	1.12	1.68	0.63	1.26	2.11	3.81	1.72	1.71	1,397.70	.22	735.18	.13	187.49	.04
Biology/science teacher	1.12	1.34	0.61	0.97	2.36	2.92	1.85	1.58	1,321.84	.21	101.74	.02	18.86	<.01
… had contact with the child?									**84.60**	**.07**	**152.45**	**.12**	**4.99**	**<.01**
Math teacher	1.80	2.31	1.29	1.62	2.79	2.93	1.90	1.89	287.10	.05	46.65	<.01	14.87	<.01
Language arts teacher	1.92	2.27	1.30	1.57	2.94	2.95	1.88	1.89	328.90	.06	15.02	<.01	13.34	<.01
English teacher	1.32	2.29	0.92	1.57	2.03	2.88	1.67	1.86	193.70	.04	384.62	.07	*1.60*	
Biology/science teacher	1.46	1.71	1.06	1.30	2.33	2.35	1.79	1.64	314.34	.06	9.32	<.01	7.42	<.01
… had contact with a parent?									**10.39**	**<.01**	**239.04**	**.17**	**22.57**	**.02**
Math teacher	2.11	1.44	1.35	1.00	2.41	1.26	1.60	0.76	*3.64*		781.48	.13	55.84	.01
Language arts teacher	2.24	1.44	1.38	0.97	2.50	1.29	1.59	0.80	*3.25*		951.46	.15	40.67	<.01
English teacher	1.42	1.43	1.00	0.99	1.77	1.23	1.39	0.72	7.03	<.01	84.17	.02	89.64	.02
Biology/science teacher	1.63	1.20	1.20	0.72	2.07	1.11	1.52	0.52	34.52	<.01	575.07	.10	83.85	.02

Note. All F values p < .05; exceptions are written in italic letters. df: 44,684–15,855. Values written in bold describe the results of the multivariate analyses of variance.

Indeed, at both elementary and secondary schools, the perceived frequency by parents of all recorded distance learning activities, such as giving feedback, teaching via video conferencing, and the communication with the child, had increased statistically significant from the first lockdown to the second lockdown. However, frequencies were partly still low (see ESM 1, Supplement 3). Only 5.1% of the parents of the elementary school children said that the video conference lessons were given according to the class schedule. This was stated by 24.5% of the parents at secondary schools. Furthermore, many children had not received any distant teaching activity of high quality. For example, at both elementary (19.5%–47.1%) and secondary (24.1%–36.7%) schools, children still did not receive any feedback on their task solutions in the various subjects. In elementary schools, between 41.5% and 68.2% of the parents stated that no lessons had yet taken place via video conference in the assessed subjects (at secondary schools only between 20.1% and 42.1%), although – according to parents – both elementary (75.5%) and secondary (96.8%) schools used Internet platforms for distance learning. Although overall communication with children had also increased from the first lockdown to the second lockdown, many parents indicated that their children had not yet communicated with the teacher in any way (elementary school: 40.9%–69%; secondary schools: 41.1%–58.6%).

All descriptive statistics and bivariate correlations are displayed in ESM 1, Supplement 1 (Table E1). As assumed in Hypothesis 3, most distant teaching activities showed small- to medium-sized positive correlations with students' motivation, competent and independent learning, and learning progress during the school lockdown for elementary and secondary school students. Distant teaching activities just show negligible associations with sociodemographic variables.

Structural Equation Models

First, we tested the measurement model of the distant teaching activities (measurement model depicted in ESM 1, Supplement 2). For the elementary school sample, the model fit was good: $\chi^2(df = 366) = 1852.78, p < .001$; RMSEA = .055 (90% CI: .053; .058); CFI = .950; SRMR = .025. For secondary schools, $\chi^2(df = 366) = 1,135.42, p < .001$; RMSEA = .032 (90% CI: .030; .035); CFI = .981; SRMR = .014.

Second, we regressed students' motivation, competent and independent learning, and learning progress during the school lockdown on the different teaching activities and students' characteristics (for the results without students' characteristics and demographics, see Supplements 5 and 6 in ESM 1). In the secondary school sample, the item "providing lessons via videoconferences according to the timetable" was additionally included (in Steinmayr et al., 2021, this item was not assessed). However, we did not include it in the elementary school sample as the item barely showed variance. Table 2 displays model fit indices and correlations between residuals for elementary and secondary schools. The model fit was excellent in all models. Table 3 depicts path coefficients from all independent variables to students' motivation, competent and independent learning, and learning progress for the two samples.

In elementary schools, giving feedback, teaching via videoconferences, and communications with a parent were still positively associated with students' motivation and perceived learning progress after controlling for all other variables. Communication with the child displayed an association with these student outcomes and with competent and independent learning. Requesting solutions was negatively associated with elementary students' motivation. However, as this distant teaching activity displayed positive bivariate correlations with students' outcomes (see ESM 1, Supplement 1), this must be due to a suppression effect. Negative emotionality (negatively) and school engagement (positively) predicted all student outcomes after controlling for all other variables with the strongest effects sizes, whereas perceived math and language art competencies were only significant for students' competent and independent learning. Among the demographic and social variables, effects were only found on perceived learning progress: Parents perceived their girls and younger children to learn more. Furthermore, parents with a higher school leaving certificate and/or a migration background, as well as mothers, thought their children to have a higher learning progress during the second school lockdown.

In the secondary school, feedback, videoconferences, and communication with a child predicted all three

Table 2. Model fit indices and intercorrelations between exogenous variables for SEMs regressing distant teaching activities and students' characteristics on students' academic outcomes during the school lockdown for elementary school (ES) and secondary school (Sec)

School type	χ^2 (df)	RMSEA (CI 90%)	SRMR	CFI	$r_{resM \times resC}$	$r_{resM \times resL}$	$r_{resC \times resL}$
ES	3,752.22 (1,290)	.038 (.036–.039)	.024	.956	.520	.492	.256
Sec	3,721.72 (1,322)	.030 (.029–.031)	.022	.965	.462	584	.206

Note. resM = residual factor motivation, resC = residual factor competent and independent learning, resL = residual learning process.

Table 3. Standardized path weights (β) and standard error (SE) of the SEM regressing distant teaching activities on students' academic outcomes during the school lockdown controlling for students' school-related characteristics, socioeconomic background, and parent' and child's age and gender for secondary schools and elementary schools

	Elementary school						Secondary school					
	Motivation		CIL		Learning progress		Motivation		CIL		Learning progress	
Model	β	SE	β	SE	β	SE	β	SE	β	SE	β	SE
Distant teaching activities during the school lockdown												
Tasks	.030	.029	.020	.028	.032	.029	−.046	.056	−.078	.052	−.102	.060
Task solutions	.041	.031	.020	.029	.009	.031	.034	.038	.092*	.036	.092*	.038
Request solutions	−.069*	.034	−.061	.032	−.062	.034	−.046	.046	−.042	.044	.021	.047
Feedback	.091**	.037	.055	.035	.117***	.037	.174***	.043	.134***	.041	.152***	.044
Grading	.013	.028	−.037	.027	.008	.028	.033	.024	−.024	.024	.047	.025
Video	.077**	.031	−.020	.029	.090**	.031	.117**	.038	.153***	.037	.106***	.039
Com. child	.109***	.032	.100***	.031	.095**	.032	.119***	.030	.082**	.029	.082**	.031
Com. parent	.072*	.030	.060*	.028	.086**	.030	.060*	.026	−.024	.025	.112***	.026
Timetable							.080**	.027	.042	.026	.108***	.028
Student characteristics												
Neg. emotionality	−.138***	.032	−.211***	.030	−.092**	.032	−.135***	.029	−.122***	.027	−.019	.030
Engagement	.452***	.038	.135***	.038	.198***	.039	.443***	.032	.097***	.031	.248***	.033
Math competence	−.014	.033	.290***	.031	−.018	.033	.011	.025	.175***	.024	.017	.026
Language competence	−.025	.034	.250***	.032	−.014	.034	.007	.028	.201***	.027	.022	.029
Social background												
HSLC	.040	.027	.039	.026	.085***	.027	.040	.022	.061**	.021	.074**	.022
Migration	−.023	.026	−.038	.025	−.058*	.026	−.001	.022	−.005	.021	−.028	.022
Own room	.028	.027	−.012	.026	.009	.027	.006	.027	−.003	.028	.028	.027
Computer	.031	.026	.030	.026	−.019	.027	.002	.029	.026	.026	.011	.027
Gender and age												
Child's gender	−.004	.028	−.003	.027	.060*	.028	−.012	.023	.031	.023	−.041	.024
Child's age	−.002	.028	.024	.027	−.076**	.027	−.060**	.023	.196***	.023	−.096***	.024
Parent's gender	.006	.027	<.001	.026	.084**	.027	.001	.022	.040	.021	.096***	.022
Parent's age	.048	.029	−.010	.027	.026	.028	−.011	.024	.005	.023	−.048*	.024
R^2	.345 (.027)		.415 (.026)		.156 (.020)		.492 (.022)		.406 (.021)		.296 (.020)	

Note. CIL = competent and independent learning; tasks = sending tasks; tasks solutions = sending task solutions; request solutions = requesting students' solutions; feedback = providing feedback on students' solutions; video = teaching via videoconference; Com. Child = student–teacher communication; Com. Parent = parent–teacher communication; timetable: videoconferences according to the timetable; Neg. emotionality = negative emotionality; engagement = school engagement; math competence = competencies in math; language competence = competencies in language arts; HSLC = highest school leaving certificate; migration = migration background; own room = child has an own bedroom; computer = child has a computer/tablet during the school lockdown. Highest school leaving certificate: 0 = no or vocational track school leaving certificate, 1 = academic track school leaving certificate; migration background: 0 = no, 1 = yes; child has an own bedroom: 0 = no, 1 = yes; child has a computer/tablet: 0 = no, 1 = yes; gender: 0 = male, 1 = female.
*p ≤ .05. **p ≤ .01. ***p ≤ .001.

student outcomes at strong effect sizes in distant teaching. Furthermore, teaching all subjects (besides sports) according to the timetable incrementally contributed to the prediction of students' motivation and learning progress. Only school engagement was still positively associated with all three student outcomes after controlling for the other variables. Negative emotionality was negatively associated with students' motivation and with competent and independent learning. Students' math and language arts competencies only incrementally explained variance in students' competent and independent learning. Parents perceived their younger children to work more motivated and learn more during the second school lockdown. However, they also perceived older children to learn more independently and competently. Furthermore, parents with a higher school leaving certificate as well as mothers and younger parents thought their children to have a higher learning progress during the second school lockdown. Parents with a higher school leaving certificate additionally reported that their children learnt more independently and competently. Thus, in line with Hypothesis 4, those distant teaching activities that directly practice or involve direct forms of interpersonal feedback and communication particularly contributed to students' academic outcomes during the school lockdown. However, in line with Hypothesis 5, children's characteristics additionally contributed to students' academic outcomes during the school lockdown.

Discussion

This study contributes to current literature on learning during times of distance teaching by examining how the realization of distant teaching changed from the first school lockdown to the second school lockdown and how various features of distance teaching were related to different academic outcomes among elementary and secondary school students using parent reports.

Comparison of the First and Second Lockdowns

Our findings show that – as indicated by other studies (Wößmann et al., 2021) – the frequency of distant teaching activities increased from the first school lockdown to the second school lockdown. Thus, in contrast to other countries such as Spain (Alves et al., 2022), the situation improved in Germany. However, compared to other studies, we show a detailed picture of how often different distant teaching activities were realized in different subjects. Contact with a parent increased statistically significant from the first lockdown to the second lockdown but did not reach the effect size of a small effect. The largest effect size was found for teaching via videoconference, which might be a hint that the investments in digital devices such as teacher laptops and in educating teachers paid off in terms of more frequent videoconferences. However, although most teachers should have been able to teach via videoconferences in the second lockdown, quite a lot of teachers at secondary schools and even more at elementary schools did not do so or if just once a week.

Distant Teaching Activities and Student Outcomes

Most correlations between reported distant teaching activities and motivation, competent and independent teaching, and perceived learning progress were positive. However, different result patterns emerged between elementary and secondary schools. Distant teaching activities explained less variance in elementary student outcomes than in the secondary school. Interestingly, those distant teaching activities related most strongly to parent-reported students' outcomes during the second school lockdown that had the potential to cognitively activate students and to support learning. Thus, in line with prior findings on the first school lockdown (Schneider et al., 2021), our results also indicate that social contact and feedback matter most. Overall, less variance was explained by distant teaching activities in the elementary than in the secondary school sample (see ESM 1, Supplement 6). A possible explanation why distant teaching activities do not seem to make a great difference concerning elementary school learning are that elementary school children strive less for autonomy (Deci & Ryan, 2013) and might still need more direct instructions as their self-regulation is still developing (McClelland et al., 2018), which is less possible by distant teaching activities. Our results also showed that the provision of feedback mattered for both elementary and secondary students' motivation and learning progress. Interestingly, sending solutions only had a (positive) impact on competent and independent learning and perceived learning progress for secondary school learners. An explanation for this finding might be that adolescent learners might already have developed a certain level of self-regulation skills that enables them to compare their own solutions to the solutions that teachers have sent them, whereas younger children might still need to develop these skills of self-regulated learning. Research suggests that childhood is a sensitive period in which self-regulatory skills are shaped by contextual factors, such as schools and teachers (McClelland et al., 2018). Thus, when planning their instruction during times of distant teaching, teachers need to consider academic needs of the children in their learning groups. Our findings suggest that although adolescents can work well with prepared solutions, children need different forms of contact to their teachers such as feedback or direct communication with parents.

Students' Characteristics, Sociodemographic Variables, and Student Outcomes

A comparison of explained variance by teaching activities alone (ESM 1, Supplement 6) and teaching activities plus all covariates (Table 3) demonstrates that students' characteristics explained most variance in all students' outcomes in the elementary school and in competent and independent learning in the secondary school during homeschooling among all relevant variables. Among students' characteristics, negative emotionality and school engagement explained most variance, whereas math and language art competencies were less relevant. Parents reported sociodemographic background contributed to the prediction of students' motivation, competencies, and learning progress during homeschooling. Parents with an academic school leaving certificate reported more positive student outcomes, which is in line with various studies that demonstrated that children from low SES households suffered the most during school lockdowns (e.g., Ravens-Sieberer et al., 2022). Thus, not only do students academically benefit from their parents' academic education in regular face-to-face schooling but also during homeschooling.

Limitations

A limitation of this study was that we used a cross-sectional design. Thus, the direction of the presented relations between distant teaching activities and student outcomes is unclear. However, as previous studies longitudinally demonstrated an impact of teaching activities on students' motivation and achievement (e.g., Lazarides & Buchholz, 2019), it might well be that teachers' distant teaching activities impacted on students' academic outcomes during the school lockdown. Furthermore, common method bias might have influenced our results because parents reported the teaching methods under investigation and also reported the student outcomes. Thus, the relations that we found in our study might be overestimated due to common method bias. Additionally, we had a slight overrepresentation of academic track schools in our sample (Gymnasium), which might have affected our results when comparing elementary and secondary school students (Hypothesis 1) as mostly high-achieving students attend academic track schools. Moreover, we were not able to assess whether our data had a nested school structure because due to data protection, we were not able to ask parents which school their child was attending. Furthermore, as we carried out an online survey during school closures and did not ask students in classrooms, we also do not have any information about whether students attended the same classrooms.

Another limitation refers to the operationalization of migration background, which would have been more valid if we had referred to the language spoken at home. Finally, children's and parents' gender and age were considered in our analyses but no other variables such as socioeconomic status (besides the school leaving certificate) or parental educational level – both variables that were shown to be of relevance during distant teaching with children from less-educated families with lower economic status made less progress over time than students in higher SES schools (e.g., Segers et al., 2022). Furthermore, socially disadvantaged children also faced higher risks of worsened mental health (Ng & Ng, 2022).

Practical Implications

As the current study clearly demonstrated the importance of direct forms of contact between teachers and pupils for all age groups, and especially the younger children, the political decision to keep schools and other forms of childcare/day-care open at all costs is timely and appropriate. This will contribute not only to students' academic learning success but also to their emotional well-being and mental health – crucial factors that are strongly impaired due to the pandemic and former lockdowns (Ravens-Sieberer et al., 2022) and that will take time to recover. Regular schooling and contact with peers and friends will support such a recovery.

Electronic Supplementary Material

The electronic supplementary material is available with the online version of the article at https://doi.org/10.1027/2151-2604/a000528

ESM 1. Table E1: Descriptive statistics of all variables. Table E2: Frequencies of all distant teaching activities. Table E3: Model fit indices and intercorrelations between exogenous variables for structure equation models. Table E4: Path weights of the structure equation model (SEM) regressing distant teaching activities.

References

Alves, D., Marques, S., Cruz, J., Mendes, S. A., & Cadime, I. (2022). Remote teaching practices and learning support during COVID-19 lockdowns in Portugal: Were there changes across time? *Frontiers in Psychology, 13*, Article 963367. https://doi.org/10.3389/fpsyg.2022.963367

Betthäuser, B. A., Bach-Mortensen, A. M., & Engzell, P. (2023). A systematic review and meta-analysis of the evidence on learning during the COVID-19 pandemic. *Nature Human Behaviour, 7*(3), 375–385. https://doi.org/10.1038/s41562-022-01506-4

Breaux, R., Dunn, N. C., Langberg, J. M., Cusick, C. N., Dvorsky, M. R., & Becker, S. P. (2021). COVID-19 resulted in lower grades for male high school students and students with ADHD. *Journal of Attention Disorders, 26*(7), 1011–1017. https://doi.org/10.1177/10870547211044211

Darling-Aduana, J., Woodyard, H. T., Sass, T. R., & Barry, S. S. (2022). *Learning-mode choice, student engagement, and achievement growth during the COVID-19 pandemic.* Working Paper No. 260-0122. Retrieved from https://caldercenter.org/

publications/learning-mode-choice-student-engagement-and-achievement-growth-during-covid-19-pandemic.

Deci, E. L., & Ryan, R. M. (2013). The importance of autonomy for development and well-being. In B. W. Sokol, F. M. E. Grouzet, & U. Müller (Eds.), *Self-regulation and autonomy: Social and developmental dimensions of human conduct* (pp. 19–46). Cambridge University Press.

Enders, C. K., & Bandalos, D. L. (2001). The relative performance of full information maximum likelihood estimation for missing data in structural equation models. *Structural Equation Modeling*, 8(3), 430–457. https://doi.org/10.1207/S15328007SEM0803_5

Federal Statistical Office (2020a). *Bevölkerung mit Migrationshintergrund – Ergebnisse des Mikrozensus 2019 [Population with migration background – Results of micro census 2019]*.

Federal Statistical Office (2020b). *Pressemitteilung Nr. 223 vom 19.06.2020 [Press release of 19 June 2020]*. Retrieved from. https://www.destatis.de/DE/Presse/Pressemitteilungen/2020/06/PD20_223_12411.html

Fickermann, D., & Edelstein, B. (2020). Editorial. In D. Fickermann & B. Edelstein (Hrsg.), *"Langsam vermisse ich die Schule …". Schule während und nach der Corona-Pandemie* (S. 9–33). Waxmann. https://doi.org/10.31244/9783830992318.09

Goodboy, A. K., & Kline, R. B. (2017). Statistical and practical concerns with published communication research featuring structural equation modeling. *Communication Research Reports*, 34(1), 68–77. https://doi.org/10.1080/08824096.2016.1214121

Helm, C., & Huber, S. G. (2022). Predictors of central student learning outcomes in times of COVID-19: Students', parents', and teachers' perspectives during school closure in 2020—A multiple informant relative weight analysis. *Frontiers in Education*, 7, Article 743770. https://doi.org/10.3389/feduc.2022.743770

Heyder, A., Weidinger, A. F., Cimpian, A., & Steinmayr, R. (2020). Teachers' belief that math requires innate ability predicts lower intrinsic motivation among low-achieving students. *Learning and Instruction*, 65, Article 101220. https://doi.org/10.1016/j.learninstruc.2019.101220

Huber, S. G., & Helm, H. (2020). Lernen in Zeiten der Corona-Pandemie. Die Rolle familiärer Merkmale für das Lernen von Schüler*innen. Befunde vom Schul-Barometer in Deutschland, Österreich und der Schweiz. In D. Fickermann & B. Edelstein (Hrsg.), *"Langsam vermisse ich die Schule …." Schule während und nach der Corona-Pandemie* (S. 37–60). Waxmann. https://doi.org/10.31244/9783830992318.09

Klieme, E., Pauli, C., & Reusser, K. (2009). The Pythagoras study: Investigating effects of teaching and learning in Swiss and German mathematics classrooms. In T. Janik, & T. Seidel (Eds.), *The power of video studies in investigating teaching and learning in the classroom* (pp. 137–160). Waxmann.

König, J., Jäger-Biela, D. J., & Glutsch, N. (2020). Adapting to online teaching during COVID-19 school closure: Teacher education and teacher competence effects among early career teachers in Germany. *European Journal of Teacher Education*, 43(4), 608–622. https://doi.org/10.1080/02619768.2020.1809650

Lazarides, R., & Buchholz, J. (2019). Student-perceived teaching quality: How is it related to different achievement emotions in mathematics classrooms? *Learning and Instruction*, 61, 45–59. https://doi.org/10.1016/j.learninstruc.2019.01.001

Lorenz, C. (2011). *Diagnostische Kompetenz von Grundschullehrkräften: strukturelle Aspekte und Bedingungen* (Vol. 9). University of Bamberg Press.

Lorenz, R., Brüggemann, T., & McElvany, N. (2020). *Unterricht während der Corona-Pandemie. Zweiter Ergebnisbericht der bundesweiten Lehrkräftebefragung. Ergebnisse, Teil II: "Wohlbefinden der Lehrkräfte"*. Institut für Schulentwicklungsforschung (IFS). Zugriff am 30.10.2022. Verfügbar unter: https://ifs.ep.tu-dortmund.de/forschung/projekte-am-ifs/abgeschlossene-projekte/corona-u/

Ludewig, U., Kleinkorres, R., Schaufelberger, R., Schlitter, T., Lorenz, R., König, C., Frey, A., & McElvany, N. (2022). COVID-19 pandemic and student reading achievement: Findings from a school panel study. *Frontiers in Psychology*, 13, Article 876485. https://doi.org/10.3389/fpsyg.2022.876485

May, I., & Hoerl, L. (2022). The impact of distance learning on parental stress during the second COVID-19 lockdown in Germany. *The Family Journal*. Advance online publication. https://doi.org/10.1177/10664807221131011

McClelland, M., Geldhof, J., Morrison, F., Gestsdóttir, S., Cameron, C., Bowers, E., Duckworth, A., Little, T., & Grammer, J. J. (2018). Self-regulation. In N. Halfon, C. B. Forrest, R. M. Lerner, & E. M. Faustmann (Eds.), *Handbook of life course health development* (pp. 275–298). Springer.

Muthén, L. K., & Muthén, B. O. (1998–2015). *Mplus (Version 6.12) [Computer software]*. Author.

Ng, C. S. M., & Ng, S. S. L. (2022). Impact of the COVID-19 pandemic on children's mental health: A systematic review. *Frontiers in Psychiatry*, 13, Article 975936. https://doi.org/10.3389/fpsyt.2022.975936

Panchal, U., Salazar de Pablo, G., Franco, M., Moreno, C., Parellada, M., Arango, C., & Fusar-Poli, P. (2021). The impact of COVID-19 lockdown on child and adolescent mental health: Systematic review. *European Child and Adolescence Psychiatry*, 1–27. https://doi.org/10.1007/s00787-021-01856-w

Pianta, R. C., & Hamre, B. K. (2009). Conceptualization, measurement, and improvement of classroom processes: Standardized observation can leverage capacity. *Educational Researcher*, 38(2), 109–119. https://doi.org/10.3102/0013189X09332374

Ravens-Sieberer, U., Erhart, M., Devine, J., Gilbert, M., Reiss, F., Barkmann, C., Siegel, N., Simon, A., Hurrelmann, K., Schlack, R., Hölling, H., Wieler, L. H., & Kaman, A. (2022). Child and adolescent mental health during the COVID-19 pandemic: Results of the three-wave longitudinal COPSY study. *Journal of Adolescent Health*, 71(5), 570–578. https://doi.org/10.1016/j.jadohealth.2022.06.022

Schneider, R., Sachse, K. A., Schipolowski, S., & Enke, F. (2021). Teaching in times of COVID-19: The evaluation of distance teaching in elementary and secondary schools in Germany. *Frontiers in Education*, 6, Article 702406. https://doi.org/10.3389/feduc.2021.702406

Segers, E., In 't Zandt, M., Stoep, J., Daniels, L., Roelofs, J., & Gubbels, J. (2022). Differential effects and success stories of distance education in Covid-19 lockdowns on the development of reading comprehension in primary schools. *Reading and Writing*, 36(2), 377–400. https://doi.org/10.1007/s11145-022-10369-0

Seitz, W., & Rausche, A. (2019). *Persönlichkeitsfragebogen für Kinder zwischen 9 und 14 Jahren [Personality questionnaire for children between the age of 9 and 14]* (5th ed.). Hogrefe.

Skinner, E. A., Kindermann, T. A., & Furrer, C. J. (2008). A motivational perspective on engagement and disaffection: Conceptualization and assessment of children's behavioral and emotional participation in academic activities in the classroom. *Educational and Psychological Measurement*, 69(3), 493–525. https://doi.org/10.1177/0013164408323233

Sliwka, A., & Klopsch, B. (2020). Disruptive innovation! In D. Fickermann & B. Edelstein (Hrsg.), *"Langsam vermisse ich die Schule …". Schule während und nach der Corona-Pandemie* (S. 216–229). Waxmann. https://doi.org/10.31244/9783830992318.09

Steinmayr, R., Dinger, F. C., & Spinath, B. (2012). Motivation as a mediator of social disparities in academic achievement. *European Journal of Personality*, 26(3), 335–349. https://doi.org/10.1002/per.842

Steinmayr, R., Lazarides, R., Weidinger, A. F., & Christiansen, H. (2021). Teaching and learning during the first COVID-19 school lockdown: Realization and associations with parent-perceived students' academic outcomes. *Zeitschrift für Pädagogische Psychologie*, *35*(2–3), 85–106. https://doi.org/10.1024/1010-0652/a000306

Steinmayr, R., Paschke, P., & Wirthwein, L. (2022). Elementary school students' subjective well-being before and during the COVID-19 pandemic: A longitudinal study. *Journal of Happiness Studies*, *23*(6), 2985–3005. https://doi.org/10.1007/s10902-022-00537-y

Steinmayr, R., Weidinger, A. F., & Wigfield, A. (2018). Does students' grit predict their school achievement above and beyond their personality, motivation, and engagement? *Contemporary Educational Psychology*, *53*, 106–122. https://doi.org/10.1016/j.cedpsych.2018.02.004

Voss, T., & Wittwer, J. (2020). Unterricht in Zeiten von Corona: Ein Blick auf die Herausforderungen aus der Sicht von Unterrichts- und Instruktionsforschung. *Unterrichtswissenschaft*, *48*, 601–627. https://doi.org/10.1007/s42010-020-00088-2

Wendt, H., Bos, W., Goy, M., & Jusufi, D. (2017). *TIMSS 2015. Skalenhandbuch zur Dokumentation der Erhebungsinstrumente und Arbeit mit den Datensätzen*. Waxmann.

Wößmann, L., Freundl, V., Grewenig, E., Lergetporer, P., Werner, K., & Zierow, L. (2021). Bildung erneut im Lockdown: Wie verbrachten Schulkinder die Schulschließungen Anfang 2021? *ifo Schnelldienst*, *74*(5), 36–52.

History

Received October 31, 2022
Revision received March 28, 2023
Accepted March 30, 2023
Published online July 18, 2023

Acknowledgments

We thank Selina Engelhardt and Sven Jansen for their support in creating the online questionnaire and in data collection. Furthermore, we thank all parents who found time to participate in our study despite homeschooling their kids and their other duties.

Publication Ethics

The project is in accordance with established ethical guidelines for psychological research. The study was approved by the local review board at Philipps University Marburg. All participants provided written informed consent in accordance with the Declaration of Helsinki and its later amendments. Participation was voluntary.

Funding

Open access publication enabled by TU Dortmund University, Germany.

ORCID

Ricarda Steinmayr
 https://orcid.org/0000-0002-0294-1045
Hanna Christiansen
 https://orcid.org/0000-0002-8104-0711

Ricarda Steinmayr
Department of Psychology
TU Dortmund University
Emil-Figge-Straße 50
44227 Dortmund
Germany
ricarda.steinmayr@tu-dortmund.de

Original Article

Changes in Teachers' Perceptions of School Quality During COVID-19

Findings From a Longitudinal Study Based on Propensity Score Balancing

Christoph Helm[1,2] and Stephan Gerhard Huber[1,2]

[1]Linz School of Education, Johannes Kepler University, Linz, Austria
[2]Institute for the Economics and Management of Education, Teacher University Zug, Switzerland

Abstract: The COVID-19 pandemic brought forth unique challenges for schools, requiring a sudden shift to remote learning. However, there have been no empirical studies examining the effects of the pandemic on school quality. This study aims to address this research gap by examining teacher data from a longitudinal study ($n = 2,616$ teachers in 120 schools in Germany) on various aspects of school quality. Using multiple-group multiple-indicator univariate latent change score modeling based on latent covariate propensity score balancing, we investigate whether COVID-19 impacted school quality – that is, school climate, collective teacher efficacy, teacher cooperation, and distributed leadership. With a few exceptions, we could not detect significant differences in the development of teachers' perceptions of school quality during the pandemic compared to developments that occurred prior to the pandemic. For example, adaptive teaching increased more than before the pandemic, while social support between teachers decreased more than before the pandemic.

Keywords: school climate, collective teacher efficacy, teacher cooperation, distributed leadership, structural equation modeling

The COVID-19 pandemic has resulted in widespread school closures around the world. Numerous studies have documented the negative impact of these closures on students' learning time, academic achievement (e.g., Betthäuser et al., 2023; Daumiller et al., 2023, this issue), and psychosocial well-being (e.g., Daumiller et al., 2023, this issue; Schlack et al., 2020). In contrast, there is limited knowledge on the impact of the crisis on aspects of school quality, such as school climate, collective teacher efficacy, teacher cooperation, and distributed leadership.

On the one hand, losses in school quality are plausible given that the pandemic caught schools off guard, and teachers had no time to prepare for the shift to distance and online learning. Moreover, many teachers lacked the digital competencies required to maintain previous school quality levels during the pandemic (e.g., König et al., 2020). As a result, it is expected that aspects of school quality related to student learning, such as school climate, may have suffered during school closures. Additionally, given the multitude of new challenges, teachers may feel less capable of fulfilling their professional duties and thus report lower levels of collective teacher efficacy during this challenging time.

On the other hand, average increases in certain aspects of school quality are also plausible. For example, teacher cooperation is expected to have increased in response to the challenges of the pandemic, as it was a central source of knowledge, learning materials, and support needed for the transition to online teaching (Darling-Hammond & Hyler, 2020). The impact of the pandemic on other dimensions of school quality, such as school management, is less clear. While the pandemic placed demands on school management and may have brought it to the forefront, given the need for cohesive and unified leadership during sudden school closures, it may also have resulted in a *centralization* of leadership behavior and a departure from distributed leadership during this uncertain time.

The COVID-19 pandemic has created unprecedented challenges for schools worldwide. While there is ample evidence of the negative effects of school closures on student learning and well-being, there is limited knowledge about how the pandemic has impacted aspects of school quality. Given this lack of empirical evidence, it is imperative that future research focus on the development of school quality during the pandemic. Scholars argue, "assessing school quality during challenging times can shed light on the question of what crucial features schools need to get through a crisis well" (Haller & Novita, 2021, p. 11). This study aims to contribute to filling this research gap by analyzing teacher data from a longitudinal study. In the following sections, we review the theoretical framework and present the methodology, design, and findings of the study.

School Quality – A Theoretical Framework

In this study, teachers' perceptions of school quality were conceptualized within the framework of educational production models. These models view educational outcomes as a function of key student and school inputs. Specifically, student learning gains are produced by schools as inputs are transformed into outputs through various processes (Hanushek, 1979; Scheerens & Bosker, 1997). Ditton (2000) proposed a model that places the basic structure of inputs, processes, and outputs at different levels of the school system, including the school level where aspects of school quality reside. Despite the existence of this model, there is a lack of consensus in the literature on the specific factors that contribute to school quality. Ditton (2000) and other researchers have noted that current research on school quality presents a fragmented picture with no universally accepted list of quality characteristics. However, some overarching dimensions have been identified in the literature that are considered likely to be significant in determining school quality, including school culture (hereinafter school climate), staff development (hereinafter collective teacher efficacy), cooperation and coordination (hereinafter teacher cooperation), and school management (hereinafter distributed leadership; Ditton, 2000).

School Climate

The concept of school climate has been proposed as an important factor in determining school quality (Hoy, 1990; MacNeil et al., 2009). Contemporary meta-analyses have consistently demonstrated the significance of school climate in promoting positive student outcomes, both cognitive and noncognitive. For instance, the meta-analyses by Dulay and Karadağ (2017) and Demirtas-Zorbaz and colleagues (2021) found small to medium positive effects of school climate on student achievement. Furthermore, meta-analyses have reported positive effects of a positive school climate on reduced school violence (Steffgen et al., 2013) and problem behaviors among students (Reaves et al., 2018). These findings highlight the central role of a positive social climate in promoting students' learning. Given the documented learning losses due to COVID-19-related school closures, this becomes particularly important.

Despite the long history of research on school climate, there is still a lack of consensus on its definition and understanding (Kohl et al., 2013). In this study, we focus on three facets of school climate – *adaptive teaching at school* (ATS), *satisfaction with the school's quality* (SSQ), and *school as a living space* (SLS; i.e., extracurricular offerings) – as indicators of a supportive learning environment.

The COVID-19 pandemic has raised questions about its impact on the school climate. Regarding the three facets of school climate investigated here, early studies point to declines due to the pandemic. In German-speaking countries, the transition to distance learning during the pandemic has led to cuts in adaptive teaching (Helm et al., 2021; Letzel et al., 2020). In addition, studies from parents' (Haller & Novita, 2021) and students' perspectives (Kirsch et al., 2021) both indicate a significant drop in school satisfaction during the pandemic. Finally, recent research has found that students' participation in extracurricular activities has decreased during the pandemic, as public health restrictions have resulted in modifications or cancelations of such activities (Finnerty et al., 2021; Ilari et al., 2022; LaForge-MacKenzie et al., 2022). These findings suggest that teachers' perceptions of adaptive teaching, satisfaction with school quality, and school as a living space may also have decreased.

Collective Teacher Efficacy

The objective of teachers' continuous professional development (CPD) is to enhance their professional competencies to optimize student learning outcomes. Since the number of CPD programs completed by teachers is not a reliable predictor of student learning and, thus, not a valid measure of school quality, we focus on a construct known as *collective teacher efficacy* (CTE), which has garnered attention as a potential game changer in the field (Hattie, 2023). CTE is a school-level variable that reflects teachers' shared beliefs in their ability to positively impact students. It has been linked to school achievement in numerous studies – for example, a meta-analysis of 26 studies (Eells, 2011) showed a strong positive correlation between CTE and student achievement, with average effect sizes ranging above 0.5. Of particular interest for the present study is the work by Marcotte (2021), who compared CTE during in-person learning with CTE during remote learning due to the COVID-19 pandemic. The findings showed significant differences in two elements of CTE, student discipline and instructional strategies. Teachers reported lower success in these areas during remote instruction. Based on these findings, we hypothesized that CTE decreased during the pandemic.

Teacher Cooperation

Teacher cooperation, particularly with regard to instruction, is considered a pivotal aspect of contemporary school quality (Ditton & Müller, 2011; Scheerens & Bosker, 1997). Furthermore, it is seen as a key indicator of school development in the digital age (Gräsel et al., 2020). In the literature on teacher cooperation, much attention has been given to the concept of professional learning communities (PLCs). According to empirical studies, PLCs are linked to higher job satisfaction, self-efficacy, and the use of innovative practices (OECD, 2019). Also, research has shown that teachers who work in a collegial environment grow more rapidly in their effectiveness (Kraft & Papay, 2014). In addition, the involvement of teachers in PLCs has been shown to have a positive impact on both school and teaching quality (see Warwas & Helm, 2018, for a review). Moreover, as recently noted by scholars (Alsaleh, 2021; Darling-Hammond & Hyler, 2020; Daumiller et al., 2023, this issue; UNESCO, 2020), teacher cooperation is considered a critical capacity for school development in times of crisis, particularly in the context of the COVID-19 pandemic. The shift from in-person to remote learning has posed unprecedented challenges for schools and teachers l(e.g., preparing students to learn in a nontraditional setting, acquiring digital skills, compensating for learning losses, and fostering new forms of teacher cooperation; Darling-Hammond & Hyler, 2020; König et al., 2020). These challenges call for intensive teacher cooperation.

Given this, we hypothesize that the level of teacher cooperation – that is, *teacher cooperation for classes* (TCC) and *social support between teachers* (SST) – significantly increased during the COVID-19 pandemic. A review of the existing literature reveals that this hypothesis has yet to be systematically researched. Studies investigating teacher cooperation during the COVID-19 pandemic tend to either evaluate online Professional Learning Community programs (e.g., Rao et al., 2021) or examine the utilization of social media and learning management systems (e.g., Thorgersen & Mars, 2021). However, these studies do not provide empirical evidence regarding potential alterations in the extent of teacher cooperation as a result of the pandemic.

Distributed Leadership

The concept of distributed leadership has gained prominence in the field of educational leadership as a key characteristic of school quality (Ditton, 2000). According to researchers such as Heck and Hallinger (2009) and Hulpia and colleagues (2009), distributed leadership is characterized as a form of participative or collaborative decision-making that involves administrators, teachers, students, and parents. To operationalize distributed leadership, Hulpia and colleagues (2009) developed an inventory that measures various dimensions of distributed leadership, including supervision, support, participative decision-making, and a coherent leadership team. In this study, the focus is on *coherent leadership team* (CLT) and *participative decision-making* (PDM) as the two most central aspects of distributed leadership (Hulpia et al., 2009, 2011). CLT encompasses aspects such as goal orientation, cohesion, and role clarity that can be considered representative of distributed leadership. PDM refers to the extent to which teachers participate in the decision-making process at school and to which structures are developed to foster participation in school decisions (Hulpia & Devos, 2009).

The existing literature on the impact of distributed leadership on student learning is mixed and inconsistent. However, several studies have demonstrated that the likelihood of school improvement and organizational change increases when leadership is distributed (e.g., Harris et al., 2007). In particular, Hulpia and colleagues (2011) found that teachers' organizational commitment was significantly predicted by cooperation within the leadership team (CLT). Furthermore, Hulpia and Devos (2009) and Hulpia and colleagues (2011) have argued that an organization may benefit more from distributed leadership during times of crisis. Similarly, Tisdale (2022) and Harris and Jones (2020) noted that distributed leadership has become the default response in this crisis, requiring more school leaders to work collaboratively and creatively to address the challenges posed by COVID-19. Given that most school leaders face numerous difficulties during the pandemic, distributed leadership is seen as a necessity for survival (Harris & Jones, 2020). This view is supported by empirical studies. Adams and colleagues (2021) conducted qualitative interviews with school leaders and found that instructional and distributed leadership were deemed essential during the crisis. Meanwhile, Alene (2022) found a strong positive correlation between distributed leadership dimensions and crisis management in a study with secondary school teachers.

The Present Study

The present study aims to investigate whether changes in teachers' perceptions of school quality during the COVID-19 pandemic differed from those prior to the pandemic. The study will test two hypotheses (H1, H2) using teacher ratings from a longitudinal study.

- H1 hypothesizes that there are, on average, statistically significant losses in the dimensions of school climate and collective teacher efficacy – that is, increases are, on average, and smaller/decreases are, on average, larger in the teacher group assessed before and during COVID-19 than in the teacher group assessed prior to COVID-19.
- H2 hypothesizes that, on average, there will be increases in teacher cooperation and distributed leadership – that is, increases are, on average, and larger/decreases are, on average, smaller in the teacher group assessed before and during COVID-19 than in the teacher group assessed prior to COVID-19.

Method

Sample and Data Collection

The present study uses data from a longitudinal teacher survey in North Rhine-Westphalia, Germany, as part of a larger study investigating the effectiveness of school leadership for school development. This study represents a secondary analysis of the existing data, using it to answer different research questions related to the impact of the COVID-19 pandemic on teachers' perceptions of school quality. Data were collected at three different time points from the same sample of 2,616 teachers in 120 schools, with 1,508 teachers participating in the final wave. Teachers were recruited as part of a longitudinal school development project *impakt schulleitung* financed by Wübben Stiftung. To facilitate longitudinal data collection in an anonymous manner, we conducted an online survey using personalized surveys using Unipark software. The e-mail addresses used to invite participants were provided by the school leaders. Participation in all waves was voluntary.

The sample is divided into two groups (see Figure 1): the *COVID-19 group* and the *control group*. The COVID-19 group consisted of 32 schools (one cohort) that were assessed before and after the COVID-19-related school closures in spring 2020, with data collected in the first quarter of 2018 (Wave 1, hereinafter t1) and the fourth quarter of 2020 (Wave 3, hereinafter t3). Thus, Wave 3 assessment was conducted after schools in North Rhine-Westphalia reopened in the summer of 2020 (see https://www.land.nrw/pressemitteilung/nordrhein-westfalen-oeffnet-schulen-schrittweise-corona-betreuungsverordnung). The control group consisted of 88 schools from two cohorts, with Wave 1 assessments taking place in the first quarters of 2016 and 2017, respectively, and Wave 3 assessments conducted in the fourth quarters of 2018 and 2019, respectively. We did not use Wave 2 for the subsequent analyses because using Wave 2 would only allow us to model the change from Wave 1 to Wave 2. However, this period precedes the pandemic in both teacher groups studied; therefore, this period is irrelevant to the research question. In addition, modeling of Wave 2 would lead to more complex latent models, which increases the risk of inadmissible solutions.

Measurements

To assess various dimensions of school quality as perceived by teachers (e.g., school climate, collective teacher efficacy, teacher cooperation, and distributed leadership; see Table 1 for the subdimensions), teachers were asked to provide ratings at each wave of the study. The measurement of these constructs was based on established scales (see Table SM 1 in the supplementary material in PsychArchives at https://doi.org/10.23668/psycharchives.12581 for source citations; Helm & Huber, 2023), which were used consistently across all waves. The rating scale was a five-point Likert scale, with high values indicating a high level of agreement with the item statement. A full list of all items used in the measurement can be obtained on request from the first author of the paper.

Analytical Approach

We use the design and analysis stages of propensity score analysis proposed by Leite and colleagues (2019) to estimate the unbiased treatment effect – that is, the effect of COVID-19 on various dimensions of school quality as rated by teachers.

The Design Stage

In the design stage, the procedures involved in balancing covariates were carried out (see Leite et al., 2019). This included data preparation, selection of covariates, estimation of propensity scores (PS), implementation of PS methods, and evaluation of covariate balancing.

Data Preparation. The data preparation step involved handling missing data and accounting for the complex sampling design in the estimation of standard errors.

Handling Missing Data. Given the longitudinal design of the study, the sample reduced from t1 to t3 by about half. To account for dropout and missing values, the full information maximum likelihood method was used, as implemented in Mplus. To ensure that changes in teachers' perceptions of school quality do not represent methodological artifacts due to dropouts, we examined the extent to which the reports of teachers who participated in the survey at t1 and t3 differed from those who participated only at t1. Cohen's *d* analyses did not reveal any relevant differences – that is, sample mortality does not affect the longitudinal findings (see Helm & Huber, 2023).

Adjusting the Standard Error Estimation. In the present study, the models were estimated using a robust maximum likelihood estimation, with standard errors robust to the non-normality of observations. Moreover, we used TYPE = COMPLEX to account for the hierarchical structure of the data.

Selection of Covariates. The selection of covariates step involved identifying true confounding variables and using invariant measurement models to estimate the probability of the treatment assignment.

Identifying True Confounders. In this step, true confounders – that is, variables related to both treatment assignment and outcome – are selected. In the present study, all Wave 1 measurements of the investigated dimensions of school quality (as reported by teachers) are defined as confounders, as theory and previous research (Ditton & Müller, 2011) suggest intercorrelations. In addition, perceived teacher stress was modeled as a latent confounder. Beyond that, the following manifest confounders were selected: the share of students not reaching minimum reading standards (i.e., Level 0 or 1 in the standardized large-scale assessment of North Rhine-Westphalia – VERA3 and VERA8), school type (i.e., academic track, nonacademic track), school level (i.e., primary school, secondary school), and the heterogeneity of the student body composition, both regarding achievement and migration background.

Probability of Treatment Assignment. In the first step, the measurement model was fit and scalar measurement invariance across groups was tested. In the second step, a logistic regression to estimate the probability of treatment assignment as a function of latent covariates was fitted.

Propensity Score Estimation, Implementation, and Evaluation. Based on the invariant confounders, propensity scores (PS) were obtained using Mplus as the estimated probabilities conditional on factor scores for the latent covariates and observed covariates. To estimate the treatment effect, we implemented PS weighting, which "adjusts the distributions of the covariates for treated and untreated groups so that they are similar. Therefore, PS weights correct for the effects of overselection of participants with certain characteristics into treatment groups in the same way that sampling weights adjust for oversampling of certain groups in survey research" (Leite et al., 2019, p. 452). When implementing PS weights, we used the formula to estimate the average treatment effect for the treated (ATT; formula: PS/1-PS; Stuart, 2010). ATT represents the average effect COVID-19 had on the schools that faced the pandemic. The success of PS weighting (i.e., covariance balancing) was assessed by means of the standardized mean differences of the latent covariates between treated and untreated after the PS weighting had been applied. According to Austin (2011), as cited by Leite and colleagues (2019, p. 452), "covariate balance is adequate if the absolute values of standardized mean differences are below 0.1 *SD*s."

The Analysis Stage

In the analysis stage, the estimate of the average treatment effect on the treated group (ATT) was determined (see Leite et al., 2019). In this study, the multiple-group multiple-indicator univariate latent change score model (MG-MI-ULCSM, Kievit et al., 2018) with propensity score (PS) weights was used to estimate the ATT (Leite et al., 2019). To avoid overcomplex models that result in inadmissible estimates, a separate MG-MI-ULCSM was estimated for each of the eight school quality dimensions.

Information on the Software Used

All analyses were conducted in Mplus 8 (Muthén & Muthén, 1998–2017).

Model Fit Evaluation

To determine the model fit, common cut-off criteria were used (Hu & Bentler, 1999; Little, 2013) – Bentler's comparative fit index (CFI ≥ .90), the Tucker–Lewis index (TLI ≥ .90), the root mean square error of approximation (RMSEA ≤ .08), and the standardized root mean square residual (SRMR ≤ .08) – at both the teacher and school levels.

Measurement Invariance

In this study, we compared changes in teachers' perceptions of school quality from two waves (i.e., t1 and t3) between schools prior to and during the COVID-19 pandemic. We tested for measurement invariance to ensure that the items used equally well assessed the same constructs in both groups and in both waves. We evaluated metric invariance using the rule of thumb from Chen (2007) and Cheung and Rensvold (2002), where a decrease of no more than 0.005–0.010 units in CFI and an increase of no more than 0.015 units in RMSEA indicate metric invariance.

Results

Descriptive Statistics

The descriptive statistics are presented in Table 2. A comparison of mean values over time revealed that all dimensions of school quality, with the exception of school as a living space (SLS), exhibited statistically significant increases. However, the effect size (*d*) of these increases was negligible in all cases.

Probability of Treatment Assignment

The findings of the analysis performed in the design stages are reported in the online supplementary material. The analysis results indicate measurement-invariant confounders and outcome variables as well as an acceptable quality of covariate balancing so that the prerequisites for the application of PS weighting and further analyses in the subsequent analysis stage are met.

Hypothesis 1 – Losses in School Climate and Collective Teacher Efficacy

To test Hypothesis 1, a multiple-group structural equation modeling (SEM) – as outlined in the analysis stage section above (see also Figure 2) – was estimated for each of the eight school quality dimensions separately. The difference in the change score of the respective school quality dimension between the pre-COVID-19 (control) group and the COVID-19 (treatment) group represents the average treatment effect. The results show that the average treatment effects for the school climate dimensions were only statistically significant for adaptive teaching at school (ATS: $\delta = .239$, $SE(\delta) = .116$, $p = .039$) but neither for school as a living space (SLS: $\delta = -.006$, $SE(\delta) = .152$, $p = .969$) nor for satisfaction with school quality (SSQ: $\delta = .095$, $SE(\delta) = .113$, $p = .399$). These results indicate that COVID-19 only impacted the school climate with regard to adaptive teaching (as rated by teachers). Contrary to our expectation, the average treatment effect for collective teacher efficacy was positive and statistically significant (CTE: $\delta = .349$, $SE(\delta) = .095$, $p < .001$). Thus, teachers facing COVID-19 reported higher increases on average in CTE than teachers assessed prior to COVID-19. Given these findings, we conclude that the results do not support Hypothesis 1.

Hypothesis 2 – Increases in Teacher Cooperation and Distributed Leadership

The results from multiple-group SEM indicate that the average treatment effect for the dimensions of teacher cooperation (teacher cooperation for class, TCC, and social support between teachers, SST) and of distributed leadership (coherent leadership team, CLT, and participative decision-making, PDM) were only statistically significant for social support between teachers (TCC: $\delta = .121$, $SE(\delta) = .102$, $p = .235$; SST: $\delta = -.287$, $SE(\delta) = .102$, $p = .005$; CLT: $\delta = -.012$, $SE(\delta) = .105$, $p = .907$; PDM: $\delta = -.082$, $SE(\delta) = .127$, $p = .521$). In contrast to our expectations, social support among teachers dropped during the COVID-19 period; however, this was not the case regarding teacher cooperation for classes. These results indicate that – after covariate balancing and after controlling for t1 of the respective school quality dimension – changes in teacher cooperation for classes and indicators of distributed leadership did not differ between the pre-COVID-19 group and the COVID-19 group. Hence, given our data and analytical approach, we were not able to detect the impact of COVID-19 on teacher cooperation and leadership style in schools. Given these findings, we conclude that Hypothesis 2 is rejected.

Discussion

The present study aimed to address the research gap on the impact of the COVID-19 pandemic on the central dimensions of teacher-reported school quality (Ditton, 2000). While research on the quality of schooling during COVID-19 has primarily focused on instructional quality (e.g., Helm & Huber, 2022; Jaekel et al., 2021; Steinmayr et al., 2021), school-level aspects have been largely neglected. Our study adds to this limited knowledge by analyzing covariate-balanced longitudinal teacher data in a treatment/control group design using univariate latent difference score models (Kievit et al., 2018; Leite et al., 2019). The findings suggest that changes in teachers' perceptions of school quality during the pandemic were largely similar to those before the pandemic, except for a greater increase in adaptive teaching at school and a lesser increase in social support between teachers compared to the control group. These results not only contribute to an advanced disciplinary understanding of the pandemic's impact on our school system but also provide important information for practitioners, school administrators, education policymakers, and administrators on which features of school quality may have been most affected by the pandemic. This information can be used to guide school development projects and interventions.

The present study has revealed some surprising findings that warrant discussion in order to shed light on possible theoretical and methodological explanations, limitations of the study (e.g., the use of teacher ratings and a single-level analysis), and practical implications. We do so in the next section.

Impact of COVID-19 on Central Dimensions of Teacher-Reported School Quality

School Climate
In Hypothesis 1, we assumed COVID-19-related losses in the school climate. Based on previous COVID-19 studies reporting increased teacher stress associated with lower perceived school climate (e.g., Brion & Kiral, 2022; Gillani et al., 2022; Trinidad, 2021), limited adaptive teaching (e.g., Letzel et al., 2020), lower school satisfaction (e.g., Haller & Novita, 2021; Kirsch et al., 2021), and decreased extracurricular activities (e.g., Finnerty et al., 2021; Ilari et al., 2022; LaForge-MacKenzie et al., 2022), a loss in teachers' school climate ratings is plausible. However, we did not observe this in our study, and one possible explanation could be the way in which school climate was measured, at least in terms of the two dimensions of satisfaction with school quality (SSQ) and school as a living space (SLS). The items ask about aspects of the school that were temporarily suspended during the pandemic, such as

extracurricular activities, but nevertheless represent the fundamental characteristics of the school. As a result, teachers may have disregarded or only minimally considered the specific, short-term exceptional situation of the pandemic in their ratings. An explanation for the comparatively better development of adaptive teaching at school (ATS) during the pandemic may be that COVID-19 made student-centered teaching more necessary than ever before, and this is reflected in our findings. These efforts may have been further intensified during school reopening and catch-up programs. In particular, the educational catch-up programs in Germany had a strong focus on individual student support (Helbig et al., 2022). In addition, on reopening, it was necessary to support students from less advantaged backgrounds to regain lost ground (Maldonado & Witte, 2021). These efforts could also help explain the stronger teachers' perceptions of adaptive teaching after the pandemic.

Collective Teacher Efficacy

Many scholars (e.g., Huber & Helm, 2020) and educational authorities (e.g., the United Nations) argued that the immediate implementation of distance learning modalities during the pandemic left many teachers lacking relevant ICT skills. Moreover, Marcotte (2021) found declines in elements of collective teacher efficacy (CTE) during the pandemic. Therefore, in Hypothesis 1, we initially also expected a significant decline in CTE (next to a decline in school climate). However, the unexpected observed increase in CTE could be explained by the rapid learning of online teaching strategies through mutual support among teachers, leading to a stronger sense of collective efficacy than before the crisis. The pandemic has shown many teachers that they are capable of successfully managing unprecedented crises. This sense of competence was probably nurtured by (1) the absence of great learning losses in Germany (e.g., Depping et al., 2021), (2) the high esteem in which parents held the teaching profession (Huber et al., 2020), and (3) the positive attention and appreciation teachers received via the media (Huber et al., 2020). The successful management of the crisis in comparison to other countries could have led to an increased sense of self-efficacy among German teachers.

Teacher Cooperation

Teacher cooperation is regarded as a dimension of school quality and is vital for teacher and school development (Ditton, 2000). Particularly in times of crisis, such as the COVID-19 pandemic, it is assumed that schools with a supportive culture of cooperation will be more likely to master current challenges, such as the organization of digital instruction (e.g., Alsaleh, 2021; Darling-Hammond & Hyler, 2020). Hypothesis 2 assumed an increase in teacher cooperation during the pandemic. However, while our results suggest that the development of teacher cooperation for classes (TCC) was not impacted by COVID-19, our findings point to a less positive change in social support between teachers (SST) during the pandemic compared to before the pandemic. A possible explanation for this unexpected result may be the contact restrictions during the pandemic as well as the increased workload associated with distance learning, which limit opportunities and time for social exchange. The lack of face-to-face contact apparently also affected the social support between teachers.

Distributed Leadership

Distributed leadership became crucial during the COVID-19 crisis, as noted by Tisdale (2022) and Harris and Jones (2020). Thus, our study hypothesized that the pandemic would boost elements of distributed leadership, such as a coherent leadership team (CLT) and participative decision-making (PDM). However, our results did not support this hypothesis, as changes in distributed leadership during the pandemic were similar to those before the pandemic. While studies (Adams et al., 2021; Alene, 2022) highlight the relevance of distributed leadership for managing the COVID-19 crisis, they do not provide insight into the expected changes in leadership style during the pandemic. It may have been unrealistic to expect that school leadership would become more participative during the crisis, given the demands of crisis management, such as implementing safety measures and making quick decisions, which may not be conducive to participative leadership.

Limitations and Implications for Further Research

Our study employed a broad theoretical approach based on established educational production models (Ditton, 2000; Hanushek, 1979), which could be seen as a limitation because it neither narrows the variety of possible dimensions of school quality to relevant aspects nor does it specifically focus on relevant dimensions of school quality during times of crisis. Future research could benefit from utilizing theories that are more targeted toward understanding schools' coping strategies in times of crisis. In particular, the role of digitization as a putative key school quality characteristic (during the pandemic) should be included in future studies. Additionally, the chosen theoretical framework does not address questions regarding the variability of school quality, such as whether it is a variable construct and to what extent it is affected by crises or other predictors. More research is needed to fully understand the variability in school quality.

Our study has methodological limitations in addition to limitations regarding the theoretical framework. First, due to the small number of schools in our data set, we were not able to estimate complex multilevel latent covariate models at the school level, which would have been the more appropriate level of analysis as dimensions of school quality represent contextual variables (Marsh et al., 2009). Second, we relied on teacher self-reports, which are subject to upward bias, especially when teachers rate aspects for which they are responsible, such as teacher–student contact or the quality of teaching (Helm & Huber, 2022; Wagner et al., 2016). Future studies should include external ratings, such as students' and parents' ratings of school quality, to triangulate the findings. Third, it is unclear to what extent the sample investigated is representative of the entire teacher population in North Rhine-Westphalia. For instance, we lacked information on the social compositions of the schools. Future studies should use representative data. Finally, we want to point out that individual characteristics, such as teachers' gender and age, might influence teacher ratings of school quality (Mitchell et al., 2010) but were not controlled for in the present study.

Nevertheless, we would like to highlight the strengths of our study design. The strengths lie in the longitudinal quasitreatment/control group design with balanced data (propensity score weighting), which allows causal conclusions (albeit only cautiously).

Conclusion

The present study provides further evidence that school quality is a complex and multifaceted construct that requires further investigation. Despite our best efforts, we have only scratched the surface of our understanding of the variability, development, and predictors of school quality. Moving forward, we suggest that school quality research develops more precise operationalizations of school quality, similar to the advances made in teaching quality research, in which three basic dimensions have been established (Praetorius et al., 2018). Longitudinal studies that investigate the conditions under which school quality emerges, and can be changed, are of great importance but are still missing. Our study represents a first attempt in this regard. In conclusion, our study suggests that the widely held belief that the COVID-19 pandemic has plunged the education system into crisis may not be entirely accurate. Our findings indicate that schools can successfully maintain their previous levels of quality even in the face of unprecedented challenges, such as distance learning. These results highlight the need for further investigation into the nuanced and complex mechanisms that enable schools to adapt and respond effectively to challenging circumstances. Future studies may focus on predictors of changes in school quality (during crises). Such investigations may provide insights that can inform policies and practices for improving educational outcomes during crises. Education policy, authorities, school administrators, teachers, parents, and more all need to contribute to school quality within their means.

References

Adams, D., Cheah, K. S. L., Thien, L. M., & Md Yusoff, N. N. (2021). Leading schools through the COVID-19 crisis in a South-East Asian country. *Management in Education*. Advance online publication. https://doi.org/10.1177/08920206211037738

Alene, A. A. (2022). The influence of distributed leadership style on educational crisis management (the case of TPLF war) in government secondary schools of Bahir Dar City Administration, Ethiopia. *Management in Education*. Advance online publication. https://doi.org/10.1177/08920206221139636

Alsaleh, A. (2021). Professional learning communities for educators' capacity building during COVID-19: Kuwait educators' successes and challenges. *International Journal of Leadership in Education*. Advance online publication. https://doi.org/10.1080/13603124.2021.1964607

Austin, P. C. (2011). An introduction to propensity score methods for reducing the effects of confounding in observational studies. *Multivariate Behavioral Research*, 46(3), 399–424. https://doi.org/10.1080/00273171.2011.568786

Betthäuser, B. A., Bach-Mortensen, A. M., & Engzell, P. (2023). A systematic review and meta-analysis of the evidence on learning during the COVID-19 pandemic. *Nature Human Behaviour*. Advance online publication. https://doi.org/10.1038/s41562-022-01506-4

Brion, C., & Kiral, B. (2022). *Creating and sustaining positive school climate during COVID-19 pandemic* (p. 278). Educational Leadership Faculty Publications. https://ecommons.udayton.edu/eda_fac_pub/278

Chen, F. F. (2007). Sensitivity of goodness of fit indexes to lack of measurement invariance. *Structural Equation Modeling: A Multidisciplinary Journal*, 14(3), 464–504. https://doi.org/10.1080/10705510701301834

Cheung, G. W., & Rensvold, R. B. (2002). Evaluating goodness-of-fit indexes for testing measurement invariance. *Structural Equation Modeling: A Multidisciplinary Journal*, 9(2), 233–255. https://doi.org/10.1207/S15328007SEM0902_5

Darling-Hammond, L., & Hyler, M. E. (2020). Preparing educators for the time of COVID … and beyond. *European Journal of Teacher Education*, 43(4), 457–465. https://doi.org/10.1080/02619768.2020.1816961

Daumiller, M., Rivas, R., Schoon, I., & Lüftenegger, M. (2023). How did COVID-19 affect education and what can be learned moving forward? A systematic meta-review of systematic reviews and meta-analyses. *Zeitschrift für Psychologie*, 231(3), 177–191. https://doi.org/10.1027/2151-2604/a000527

Demirtas-Zorbaz, S., Akin-Arikan, C., & Terzi, R. (2021). Does school climate that includes students' views deliver academic achievement? A multilevel meta-analysis. *School Effectiveness and School Improvement*, 32(4), 543–563. https://doi.org/10.1080/09243453.2021.1920432

Depping, D., Lücken, M., Musekamp, F., & Thonke, F. (2021). Kompetenzstände Hamburger Schüler*innen vor und während der Corona-Pandemie. In D. Fickermann, & B. Edelstein (Eds.), *Schule während der Corona-Pandemie: Neue Ergebnisse und Überblick über ein dynamisches Forschungsfeld* (pp. 51–79). Waxmann. https://doi.org/10.31244/9783830993315.03

Ditton, H. (2000). Qualitätskontrolle und Qualitätssicherung in Schule und Unterricht. *Zeitschrift für Pädagogik, Beiheft, 41*, 73–92. https://doi.org/10.25656/01:8486

Ditton, H., & Müller, A. (2011). Schulqualität. In H. Reinders, H. Ditton, C. Gräsel, & B. Gniewosz (Eds.), *Lehrbuch. Empirische Bildungsforschung. Gegenstandsbereiche* (pp. 99–111). Verlag für Sozialwissenschaften. https://doi.org/10.1007/978-3-531-93021-3_9

Dulay, S., & Karadağ, E. (2017). The effect of school climate on student achievement. In E. Karadağ (Ed.), *The factors effecting student achievement: Meta-analysis of empirical studies* (pp. 199–213). Springer. https://doi.org/10.1007/978-3-319-56083-0_12

Eells, R. J. (2011). Meta-analysis of the relationship between collective teacher efficacy and student achievement. *Dissertations, 133*. https://ecommons.luc.edu/luc_diss/133

Finnerty, R., Marshall, S. A., Imbault, C., & Trainor, L. J. (2021). Extracurricular activities and well-being: Results from a survey of undergraduate university students during COVID-19 lockdown restrictions. *Frontiers in Psychology, 12*, Article 647402. https://doi.org/10.3389/fpsyg.2021.647402

Gillani, A., Dierst-Davies, R., Lee, S., Robin, L., Li, J., Glover-Kudon, R., Baker, K., & Whitton, A. (2022). Teachers' dissatisfaction during the COVID-19 pandemic: Factors contributing to a desire to leave the profession. *Frontiers in Psychology, 13*, Article 940718. https://doi.org/10.3389/fpsyg.2022.940718

Gräsel, C., Schledjewski, J., & Hartmann, U. (2020). Implementation digitaler Medien als Schulentwicklungsaufgabe. *Zeitschrift für Pädagogik, 66*(2), 208–224. https://doi.org/10.25656/01:23629

Haller, T., & Novita, S. (2021). Parents' perceptions of school support during COVID-19: What satisfies parents? *Frontiers in Education, 6*, Article 700441. https://doi.org/10.3389/feduc.2021.700441

Hanushek, E. A. (1979). Conceptual and empirical issues in the estimation of educational production functions. *The Journal of Human Resources, 14*(3), 351–388. https://doi.org/10.2307/145575

Harris, A., & Jones, M. (2020). COVID-19 – school leadership in disruptive times. *School Leadership & Management, 40*(4), 243–247. https://doi.org/10.1080/13632434.2020.1811479

Harris, A., Leithwood, K., Day, C., Sammons, P., & Hopkins, D. (2007). Distributed leadership and organizational change: Reviewing the evidence. *Journal of Educational Change, 8*(4), 337–347. https://doi.org/10.1007/s10833-007-9048-4

Hattie, J. (2023). *Collective teacher efficacy (CTE) according to John Hattie*. https://visible-learning.org/2018/03/collective-teacher-efficacy-hattie/

Heck, R. H., & Hallinger, P. (2009). Assessing the contribution of distributed leadership to school improvement and growth in math achievement. *American Educational Research Journal, 46*(3), 659–689. https://doi.org/10.3102/0002831209340042

Helbig, M., Edelstein, B., Fickermann, D., & Zink, C. (2022). *Aufholen nach Corona? Maßnahmen der Länder im Kontext des Aktionsprogramms von Bund und Ländern*. Waxmann. https://doi.org/10.31244/9783830996033

Helm, C., & Huber, S. G. (2022). Predictors of central student learning outcomes in times of COVID-19: Students', parents', and teachers' perspectives during school closure in 2020—A multiple informant relative weight analysis. *Frontiers in Education, 7*, Article 743770. https://doi.org/10.3389/feduc.2022.743770

Helm, C., & Huber, S. G. (2023). Supplemental materials to "Changes in teachers' perceptions of school quality during COVID-19: Findings from a longitudinal study based on propensity score balancing". https://doi.org/10.23668/psycharchives.12581

Helm, C., Huber, S., & Loisinger, T. (2021). Was wissen wir über schulische Lehr-Lern-Prozesse im Distanzunterricht während der Corona-Pandemie? – Evidenz aus Deutschland, Österreich und der Schweiz. *Zeitschrift für Erziehungswissenschaft, 24*(2), 237–311. https://doi.org/10.1007/s11618-021-01000-z

Hoy, W. K. (1990). Organizational climate and culture: A conceptual analysis of the school workplace. *Journal of Educational and Psychological Consultation, 1*(2), 149–168. https://doi.org/10.1207/s1532768xjepc0102_4

Hu, L., & Bentler, P. M. (1999). Cutoff criteria for fit indexes in covariance structure analysis: Conventional criteria versus new alternatives. *Structural Equation Modeling, 6*(1), 1–55. https://doi.org/10.1080/10705519909540118

Huber, S. G., Günther, P. S., Schneider, N., Helm, C., Schwander, M., Schneider, J., & Pruitt, J. (2020). *COVID-19 und aktuelle Herausforderungen in Schule und Bildung*. Waxmann. https://doi.org/10.31244/9783830942160

Huber, S. G., & Helm, C. (2020). COVID-19 and schooling: Evaluation, assessment and accountability in times of crises—Reacting quickly to explore key issues for policy, practice and research with the school barometer. *Educational Assessment, Evaluation and Accountability, 32*(2), 237–270. https://doi.org/10.1007/s11092-020-09322-y

Hulpia, H., & Devos, G. (2009). Exploring the link between distributed leadership and job satisfaction of school leaders. *Educational Studies, 35*(2), 153–171. https://doi.org/10.1080/03055690802648739

Hulpia, H., Devos, G., & Rosseel, Y. (2009). Development and validation of scores on the distributed leadership inventory. *Educational and Psychological Measurement, 69*(6), 1013–1034. https://doi.org/10.1177/0013164409344490

Hulpia, H., Devos, G., & van Keer, H. (2011). The relation between school leadership from a distributed perspective and teachers' organizational commitment. *Educational Administration Quarterly, 47*(5), 728–771. https://doi.org/10.1177/0013161X11402065

Ilari, B., Cho, E., Li, J., & Bautista, A. (2022). Perceptions of parenting, parent–child activities and children's extracurricular activities in times of COVID-19. *Journal of Child and Family Studies, 31*(2), 409–420. https://doi.org/10.1007/s10826-021-02171-3

Jaekel, A.-K., Scheiter, K., & Göllner, R. (2021). Distance teaching during the COVID-19 crisis: Social connectedness matters most for teaching quality and students' learning. *AERA Open, 7*, Article 233285842110520. https://doi.org/10.1177/23328584211052050

Kievit, R. A., Brandmaier, A. M., Ziegler, G., van Harmelen, A.-L., de Mooij, S. M., Moutoussis, M., Goodyer, I. M., Bullmore, E., Jones, P. B., Fonagy, P., Lindenberger, U., & Dolan, R. J. (2018). Developmental cognitive neuroscience using latent change score models: A tutorial and applications. *Developmental Cognitive Neuroscience, 33*, 99–117. https://doi.org/10.1016/j.dcn.2017.11.007

Kirsch, C., Engel de Abreu, P. M. J., Neumann, S., & Wealer, C. (2021). Practices and experiences of distant education during the COVID-19 pandemic: The perspectives of six- to sixteen-year-olds from three high-income countries. *International Journal of Educational Research Open, 2*, Article 100049. https://doi.org/10.1016/j.ijedro.2021.100049

Kohl, D., Recchia, S., & Steffgen, G. (2013). Measuring school climate: An overview of measurement scales. *Educational Research, 55*(4), 411–426. https://doi.org/10.1080/00131881.2013.844944

König, J., Jäger-Biela, D. J., & Glutsch, N. (2020). Adapting to online teaching during COVID-19 school closure: Teacher education and teacher competence effects among early career teachers in Germany. *European Journal of Teacher Education, 43*(4), 608–622. https://doi.org/10.1080/02619768.2020.1809650

Kraft, M. A., & Papay, J. P. (2014). Can professional environments in schools promote teacher development? Explaining heterogeneity in returns to teaching experience. *Educational Evaluation* and *Policy Analysis*, *36*(4), 476–500. https://doi.org/10.3102/0162373713519496

LaForge-MacKenzie, K., Tombeau Cost, K., Tsujimoto, K. C., Crosbie, J., Charach, A., Anagnostou, E., Birken, C. S., Monga, S., Kelley, E., Burton, C. L., Nicolson, R., Georgiades, S., & Korczak, D. J. (2022). Participating in extracurricular activities and school sports during the COVID-19 pandemic: Associations with child and youth mental health. *Frontiers in Sports and Active Living*, *4*, Article 936041. https://doi.org/10.3389/fspor.2022.936041

Leite, W. L., Stapleton, L. M., & Bettini, E. F. (2019). Propensity score analysis of complex survey data with structural equation modeling: A tutorial with Mplus. *Structural Equation Modeling: A Multidisciplinary Journal*, *26*(3), 448–469. https://doi.org/10.1080/10705511.2018.1522591

Letzel, V., Pozas, M., & Schneider, C. (2020). Energetic students, stressed parents, and nervous teachers: A comprehensive exploration of inclusive homeschooling during the COVID-19 crisis. *Open Education Studies*, *2*, 159–170. https://doi.org/10.1515/edu-2020-0122

Little, T. D. (2013). *Longitudinal structural equation modeling*. Guilford Press. http://site.ebrary.com/lib/subhamburg/Doc?id=10664545

MacNeil, A. J., Prater, D. L., & Busch, S. (2009). The effects of school culture and climate on student achievement. *International Journal of Leadership in Education*, *12*(1), 73–84. https://doi.org/10.1080/13603120701576241

Maldonado, J. E., & Witte, K. de (2021). The effect of school closures on standardised student test outcomes. *British Educational Research Journal*. *48*(1), 49–94. https://doi.org/10.1002/berj.3754

Marcotte, K. E. (2021). *School climate and collective teacher efficacy in rural elementary schools during in-person and remote instruction*. Plymouth State University.

Marsh, H. W., Lüdtke, O., Robitzsch, A., Trautwein, U., Asparouhov, T., Muthén, B., & Nagengast, B. (2009). Doubly latent models of school contextual effects: Integrating multilevel and structural equation approaches to control measurement and sampling error. *Multivariate Behavioral Research*, *44*(6), 764–802. https://doi.org/10.1080/00273170903333665

Mitchell, M. M., Bradshaw, C. P., & Leaf, P. J. (2010). Student and teacher perceptions of school climate: A multilevel exploration of patterns of discrepancy. *The Journal of School Health*, *80*(6), 271–279. https://doi.org/10.1111/j.1746-1561.2010.00501.x

Muthén, L. K., & Muthén, B. O. (1998–2017). *Mplus user's guide* (8th edn).

OECD (2019). *TALIS 2018 Technical report*. https://www.oecd.org/education/talis/TALIS_2018_Technical_Report.pdf

Praetorius, A.-K., Klieme, E., Herbert, B., & Pinger, P. (2018). Generic dimensions of teaching quality: The German framework of Three Basic Dimensions. *ZDM*, *50*(3), 407–426. https://doi.org/10.1007/s11858-018-0918-4

Rao, A. E., Koval, J., Grossman, S., Boice, K. L., Alemda, M., & Usselman, M. (2021). Building teacher community during a summer of crisis: STEAM professional development in 2020. *The Journal of STEM Outreach*, *4*(4), 1–9. https://doi.org/10.15695/jstem/v4i4.07

Reaves, S., McMahon, S. D., Duffy, S. N., & Ruiz, L. (2018). The test of time: A meta-analytic review of the relation between school climate and problem behavior. *Aggression and Violent Behavior*, *39*, 100–108. https://doi.org/10.1016/j.avb.2018.01.006

Scheerens, J., & Bosker, R. J. (1997). *The foundations of educational effectiveness*. Pergamon.

Schlack, R., Neuperdt, L., Hölling, H., de Bock, F., Ravens-Sieberer, U., Mauz, E., Wachtler, B., & Beyer, A.-K. (2020). Auswirkungen des COVID-19-Pandemiegeschehens und behördlicher Infektionsschutzmaßnahmen auf die psychische Gesundheit von Kindern und Jugendlichen. https://doi.org/10.25646/7173

Steffgen, G., Recchia, S., & Viechtbauer, W. (2013). The link between school climate and violence in school: A meta-analytic review. *Aggression and Violent Behavior*, *18*(2), 300–309. https://doi.org/10.1016/j.avb.2012.12.001

Steinmayr, R., Lazarides, R., Weidinger, A. F., & Christiansen, H. (2021). Teaching and learning during the first COVID-19 school lockdown: Realization and associations with parent-perceived students' academic outcomes. *Zeitschrift Für Pädagogische Psychologie*, *35*(2–3), 85–106. https://doi.org/10.1024/1010-0652/a000306

Stuart, E. A. (2010). Matching methods for causal inference: A review and a look forward. *Statistical Science: A Review Journal of the Institute of Mathematical Statistics*, *25*(1), 1–21. https://doi.org/10.1214/09-sts313

Thorgersen, K. A., & Mars, A. (2021). A pandemic as the mother of invention? Collegial online collaboration to cope with the COVID-19 pandemic. *Music Education Research*, *23*(2), 225–240. https://doi.org/10.1080/14613808.2021.1906216

Tisdale, V. (2022). The art of leadership in times of crisis. *Dissertations*, *437*. https://digitalcommons.umassglobal.edu/edd_dissertations/437.

Trinidad, J. E. (2021). Teacher satisfaction and burnout during COVID-19: What organizational factors help? *International Journal of Leadership in Education*. https://doi.org/10.1080/13603124.2021.2006795

UNESCO (2020). *COVID-19 impact on education*. https://en.unesco.org/covid19/educationresponse

Wagner, W., Göllner, R., Werth, S., Voss, T., Schmitz, B., & Trautwein, U. (2016). Student and teacher ratings of instructional quality: Consistency of ratings over time, agreement, and predictive power. *Journal of Educational Psychology*, *108*(5), 705–721. https://doi.org/10.1037/edu0000075

Warwas, J., & Helm, C. (2018). Professional learning communities among vocational school teachers: Profiles and relations with instructional quality. *Teaching and Teacher Education*, *73*, 43–55. https://doi.org/10.1016/j.tate.2018.03.012

History

Received October 15, 2022
Revision received March 14, 2023
Accepted March 21, 2023
Published online July 18, 2023

Authorship

Christoph Helm, writing – original draft, writing – review & editing; data cleaning and statistical analysis; Stephan Huber, conceptualization, data collection. All authors approved the final version of the article.

Open Data

The supplementary material is available online in PsychArchives at https://doi.org/10.23668/psycharchives.12581 (Helm & Huber, 2023).

ORCID

Christoph Helm
https://orcid.org/0000-0001-5854-4500

Christoph Helm

Linz School of Education
Johannes Kepler University
Altenberger Straße 68
4040 Linz
Austria
christoph.helm@jku.at

Appendix

See Figures 1 and 2 and Tables 1 and 2.

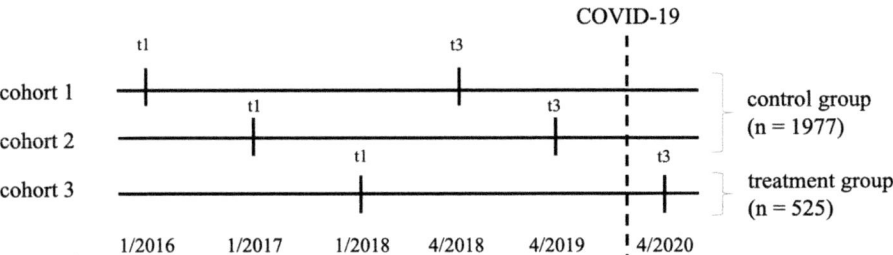

Figure 1. Measurement waves in the control and treatment groups. *Note.* Numbers before the slash indicate the quarter.

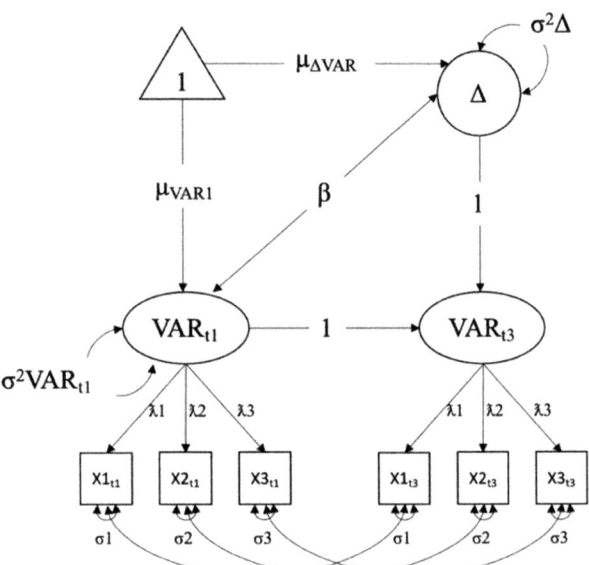

Figure 2. Multiple-indicator univariate latent change score model. *Note.* We assume scalar measurement invariance and correlated residual errors over time. VAR = school quality dimension.

Table 1. Scale information of study measures

Dimension	Nos.	Sample item
School climate		
Adaptive teaching at school (ATS)	5	At our school, the lessons are flexibly adapted to learning groups with different prerequisites by means of internal differentiation measures.
Satisfaction with school quality (SSQ)	5	I am very satisfied with the quality of teaching at our school.
School as a living space (SLS)	4	There is a wide range of cultural activities at our school (school and sports festivals, theater, music performances, etc.).
Collective teacher efficacy		
Collective teacher efficacy (CTE)	4	I am confident that our faculty can meet unexpected challenges.
Teacher cooperation		
Teacher cooperation for classes (TCC)	5	We have multidisciplinary cooperation based on common themes.
Social support between teachers (SST)	4	There are enough people in my college with whom I have a really good relationship.
Distributed leadership		
Coherent leadership team (CLT)	10	The leadership team supports the goals we like to attain with our school.
Participative decision-making (PDM)	6	We have adequate involvement in decision-making.
Additional confounders		
School type	1	Meta data
School level	1	Meta data
VERA (achievement)	—	Meta data
Leadership team member	1	Are you member of the steering committee, school-level committee, and/or faculty committee?
Heterogeneity (migration)	1	At our school we have a decidedly heterogeneous student body in terms of migration background.
Heterogeneity (achievement)	1	At our school we have a distinctly heterogeneous student body in terms of ability.
Teacher stress	4	I often feel overwhelmed.

Table 2. Descriptive statistics and reliability of the study measures

Dimension	n	t1			n	t3			p value	d
		M	SD	α		M	SD	α		
School climate										
ATS	2,543	3.589	.795	.839	1,470	3.676	0.802	.855	.001	−.109
SSQ	2,489	3.514	.814	.876	1,442	3.574	0.796	.877	.025	−.074
SLS	2,506	3.427	.795	.560	1,438	3.470	0.838	.659	.110	−.054
Collective teacher efficacy										
CTE	2,596	3.723	.813	.903	1,508	3.802	0.827	.913	.003	−.097
Teacher cooperation										
TCC	2,394	3.364	.879	.823	1,324	3.495	0.867	.825	<.001	−.150
SST	2,394	3.364	.879	.823	1,324	3.495	0.867	.825	<.001	−.150
Distributed leadership										
CLT	2,364	3.683	.934	.955	1,330	3.805	0.921	.960	<.001	−.132
PDM	2,307	3.438	.867	.881	1,268	3.592	0.849	.878	<.001	−.180
Additional confounders										
School type	2,616	.195	.396	—	—	—	—	—	—	—
School level	2,616	.182	.386	—	—	—	—	—	—	—
VERA (achievement)	2,616	24.458	15.989	—	—	—	—	—	—	—
Leadership team member	2,616	.254	.435	—	—	—	—	—	—	—
Heterogeneity (migration)	2,538	4.295	1.098	—	—	—	—	—	—	—
Heterogeneity (achievement)	2,522	4.346	1.001	—	—	—	—	—	—	—
Teacher stress	2,609	2.850	.889	.803	—	—	—	—	—	—

Note. See Table 1 for construct abbreviations. *n* = sample size. *SD* = standard deviation. α = Cronbach's α. *d* = Cohen's *d*. *p* value and *d* refer to mean comparison between t1 and t3.

Original Article

Navigating an Uncertain Future

How Schools Can Support Career Adaptability of Young People in the Aftermath of the COVID-19 Pandemic

Ingrid Schoon and Golo Henseke

Institute of Education (IoE), University College London (UCL), University of London, UK

Abstract: Young people navigate an increasingly uncertain and precarious employment market. They have to mobilise and use psychosocial resources necessary to adapt to a changing career landscape and employment opportunities. Guided by career development theories, this study asks if school-based career preparation activities can support the development of career adaptability and career-related cognitions of young people in the aftermath of the COVID-19 pandemic. The research draws on a nationally representative sample of 16–25 year-olds who participated in the Youth Economic Activity and Health (YEAH) online survey conducted in the UK between May 2021 and May 2022 (n = 4040). The findings highlight the malleability of career adaptability and the importance of school-based career preparation activities in supporting adaptive career-related cognitions as well as life satisfaction among young people in times of economic uncertainty and upheaval.

Keywords: career adaptability, uncertainty, life satisfaction, school-based career preparation activity, young people

Can education institutions help young people to adjust to a changing career landscape? Preparing for the transition from education to employment is a key developmental task for young people (Marciniak et al., 2022; Savickas et al., 2009; Schoon & Heckhausen, 2019), a task that has been critically affected by the COVID-19 pandemic and the associated economic downturn. Already before the pandemic, young people had to steer their way toward an increasingly uncertain future, characterized by a changing and volatile labor market and increasing precarity (Schoon & Bynner, 2019). During the pandemic, they were disproportionally affected by recruitment freezes, lost working hours or by layoffs, and lack of opportunities for job skill learning (Engzell et al., 2021; Green et al., 2022; Henehen, 2021). These contextual developments are posing new demands on how individuals manage their career development (Akkermans et al., 2020; Rudolph et al., 2021). More generally, adapting to change and uncertainty is a central challenge of one's life course (Hartung & Cadaret, 2017; Schoon & Heckhausen, 2019). For young people, the transition into the labor market requires preparations and planning already during their studies. They need to acquire relevant psychosocial resources for managing uncertain transitions, explore possible career paths, form more specific vocational goals, and plan how to act to implement those goals (Lent & Brown, 2013). In short, young people have to develop adaptability resources that enable them to navigate changing circumstances and uncertainty (Hirschi et al., 2015; Saviackas, 2005, 2012).

The aim of this study is to assess if schools can help young people to prepare for the step into the world of work during times of economic uncertainty. We focus on the role of school-based career preparation activities as predictors of career adaptability, i.e., people's capacity to adapt to change in a fast-moving world of work, and their responses to changing conditions, such as uncertainty regarding future job chances or worries about one's career due to the COVID-19 pandemic and associated economic turmoil.

The importance of career information and guidance in the preparation for the school-to-work transition is increasingly recognized (Mann et al., 2020) and international organizations including the OECD, the European Commission, the European Training Foundation, the International Labor Organisation and UNESCO are emphasizing its relevance and benefits for inclusive development and a fairer society (Cedefop, 2021). There is however still little empirical evidence regarding the role of school-based career preparation activities in supporting career development or more generally the contextual antecedents (such as gender, ethnicity, parental background or region) of career adaptability among young people (Hirschi & Koen, 2021). Considering both the antecedents of career adaptability and associated behaviors and adaptation results, the study is guided by career development theories (Lent & Brown, 2019; Savickas, 1997; Super, 1980) taking into account the skills and competences as well as the contextual constraints and opportunities that shape career development.

© 2023 Hogrefe Publishing

In addition, we assess to what extent school-based career preparation activities, perceived career adaptability, career worries, and uncertainty relate to life satisfaction.

Career Adaptability as a Crucial Resource for Navigating an Uncertain Future

Career development theories have long recognized that careers are changing toward increasing uncertainty and instability. To effectively navigate career transitions in the face of an uncertain future and adverse conditions, individuals need to draw on a range of psychosocial resources for tackling and solving unfamiliar, complex, and ill-defined problems (Hirschi et al., 2015; Lent & Brown, 2019; Savickas, 1997; Super, 1980). Despite agreeing on the importance of self-regulatory, transactional and malleable competencies, or psychosocial resources, for adaptive career behavior, different terms and approaches are used to conceptualize these resources.

The concept of career adaptability originated from Super's career development theory (Super et al., 1996). Moving beyond a positivist trait factor conception of career, Super (1957, 1980) advanced constructivist and social constructionist perspectives, conceptualizing career as an ongoing, unfolding, evolving process of growth and change requiring individual adaptability. Super's theory is a combination of stage development and social role theory (Super et al., 1996), which posits that people progress through five stages during the career development process, including growth, exploration, establishment, maintenance, and disengagement. Super introduced the term career maturity to denote the readiness of an individual to adjust to the demands of social roles, including the role of worker (Super, 1980). The model assumes that adolescents develop career-relevant attitudes and cognitions, such as active career exploration and planning of how to reach one's goals. In the cognitive domain, this also implies that adolescents acquire and use relevant knowledge about the content and process of career decision making and about the world of work (Hartung et al., 2017). This process of career preparations involving planning, exploration and decisions about possible careers is also referred to as career readiness (Marciniak et al., 2022; Phillips & Blustein, 1994).

Emphasizing the psychosocial aspects of the career construction processes, i.e., the person–environment interactions instead of biological maturation processes, the notion of career maturity was replaced by the career adaptability construct (Super et al., 1996). Rooted within life span theory, the notion of career adaptability acknowledged that individuals must continuously adapt throughout their life course to respond effectively to changing personal needs and changing contextual demands and opportunities (Savickas et al., 2009). Within the life design paradigm, career adaptability is conceptualized as the readiness to deal with current and anticipated vocational developmental tasks, occupational transitions, and the unpredictable adjustments prompted by changes in work and working conditions (Savickas, 1997, p. 254). Effectively dealing with developmental tasks at one life stage is understood to be crucial for tackling the tasks in the next life phase and changes encountered during occupational transitions over the life span (Savickas et al., 2009).

The concept of career adaptability is understood as a psychosocial resource residing at the intersection of person-in-environment interactions, supporting individuals to plan for uncertain futures, face adverse conditions, adapt to changes in life conditions, and increase their well-being. More specifically, career adaptability is conceptualized as a multidimensional construct, comprising four dimensions: concern (career planning), control (decision-making and self-regulation), curiosity (career exploration), and career self-confidence (Savickas & Porfeli, 2012). Concern refers to the inclination of future orientation and planning ahead. Control involves increasing self-regulation through career decision-making and taking responsibility for the future. Curiosity reflects the degree to which individuals explore the world and try to acquire information about different career options. Confidence refers to problem-solving ability and perceived self-efficacy. Having higher levels of career adaptability means to have relevant psychosocial resources that enable the effective adaption to a changing social environment while also finding ways to increase the chances of achieving one's expectations (Savickas, 2005).

Career adaptability is understood as a malleable construct, which is dynamic and learnable, as for example through career education and vocational guidance (Savickas, 2012). Building on these assumptions, Lent (2013) advanced the term career preparedness, creating a bridge to social-cognitive career theories and highlighting the role of individual agency, the importance of "a healthy state of vigilance regarding threats to one's career well-being as well as alertness to resources and opportunities on which to capitalize" (Lent, 2013, p.7).

Career Adaptability, Adaptive Responses, and Life Satisfaction

The career construction model postulates that the four adaptability resources discussed above help individuals to develop adaptive behaviors or cognitions to address changing conditions (the adaptive response) – which in turn lead to desired outcomes, such as satisfaction or success that reflect a good fit between the person and the environment (Rudolph et al., 2017; Savickas & Porfeli, 2012).

There is now persistent evidence to show that career adaptability resources are associated with adaptive response, i.e., cognitions and behaviors that address changing conditions, such as career beliefs, career planning and career exploration, as well as adaptation results, i.e., outcomes such as career commitment, employability, income, or subjective well-being (Johnston, 2018; Rudolph et al., 2017), even across different cultural contexts (Chen et al., 2020). For example, individuals with greater adaptability resources reported more effective career planning and proactive skill development (Taber & Blankemeyer, 2015) as well as employability (Khalid & Ahmad, 2021; Pajic et al., 2018).

In this study, we will focus on career-related cognitions, such as career uncertainty and career worries, during a time of major upheaval. It is assumed that higher levels of career adaptability resources are associated with lower levels of uncertainty regarding future job chances or worries about one's career due to the COVID-19 pandemic and associated economic turmoil. Moreover, we assume that career-related cognitions in addition to career adaptability resources shape the evaluation of one's life overall.

Within the career construction theory, subjective well-being (SWB) is recognized as a significant outcome (Hartung & Taber, 2008; Rudolph et al., 2017; Savickas, 2005, 2012), indicating a good fit or alignment between personal needs and contextual circumstances. Previous research has shown that individuals who report higher levels of career adaptability also feel more satisfied with their career and life overall (Fiori et al., 2015; Rudolph et al., 2017a; Santilli et al., 2017, 2020; Zacher, 2014) and report better mental health (Akkermans et al., 2018). It is argued that career construction processes facilitate a process of self-understanding and a personally meaningful frame of reference that gives their lives direction, which in turn is associated with greater levels of SWB (Blustein, 1987; Super, 1993).

In this study, we assess associations between career adaptability resources, adaptive responses, and overall life satisfaction, a widely used indicator of SWB. Overall life satisfaction is understood to reflect a person's cognitive evaluation of their life as a whole based on the standards they have for a "good life" (Diener et al., 2018).

Promoting the Development of Career Adaptability Resources Through Vocational Guidance and Information

Although career adaptability has been conceptualized as a malleable construct, there is still little evidence on how career adaptability resources can be promoted through interventions (Koen et al., 2012) or contextual influences. Most previous research on the predictors of career adaptability have focused on the role of individual characteristics, such as the big five personality traits or cognitive ability (Johnston, 2018; Rudolph et al., 2017) which has led some scholars to question whether career adaptability is indeed learnable or a fairly stable personality trait (Griffin & Hesketh, 2003; Verbruggen & Sels, 2008). There is however some evidence on the effectiveness of targeted career adaptability interventions (Camussi et al., 2023; Green et al., 2020; Perdrix et al., 2012; Spur et al., 2015), including interventions targeted at school-aged children (Hirschi & Lage, 2008; Perdrix et al., 2012).

Career construction theory offers both a theoretical model of career construction and a practical model of career guidance (Savickas et al., 2009). Interventions based on the life design paradigm (Savickas, 2012) aim to foster peoples' planning, problem-solving, exploration, and decision-making. The current study focuses on the role of school-based career education and guidance offered in collaboration with employers or local business people. These career preparation activities are part of the general curriculum and are not specifically designed to promote career adaptability. Yet, it has been argued that career education and guidance offered in secondary education can provide crucial support to help young people explore and confirm their career ambitions, increase occupational information, and develop the skills and competences required to manage their career pathways (Mann et al., 2020; Robertson, 2013). This argument has to some extent been supported by evidence from international longitudinal studies on the role of school-based career guidance and its association with later employment outcomes, earnings, and career satisfaction (Covacevich et al., 2021). In this study, we ask if career guidance provided during secondary education helps young people to develop career adaptability resources, adaptive responses for tackling changing labor market conditions in the aftermath of the COVID-19 pandemic, and contribute to their life satisfaction.

The Present Study and Hypotheses

This study is guided by assumptions formulated within career construction theories (Savickas, 2012; Savickas et al., 2009; Super et al., 1996). We test a sequential mediating model of career construction (Figure 1) linking school-based career preparation activities offered in schools and colleges to manifestation of career adaptability, career-related cognitions (career uncertainty and career worries), as well as life satisfaction. Based on the assumption that career adaptability is a malleable

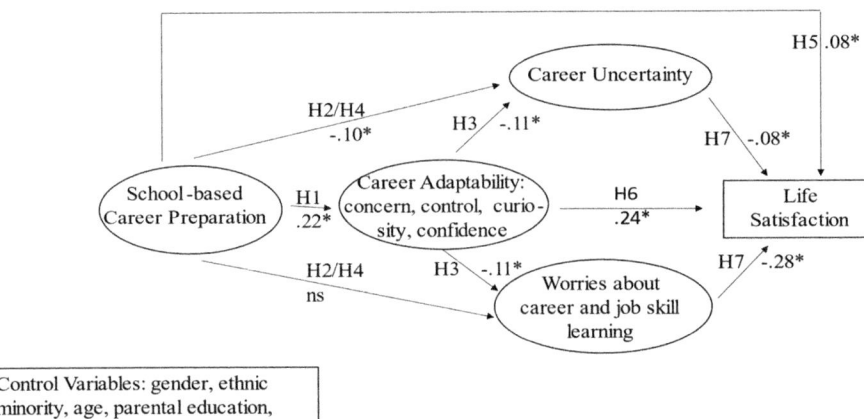

Figure 1. Sequential mediating model of career construction: sequential mediating processes linking school-based career preparation activities, career adaptability, adaptive cognitions, and life satisfaction.

construct, we expect a direct and positive effect of school-based career preparation activities on career adaptability (H1). Following the assumption that school-based career preparation activities also directly improve career-related cognitions, we expect a direct negative association between school-based career preparation activities and career worries and uncertainty (H2). Based on the assumption that career adaptability supports the development of effective career-related cognitions (adaptive response), we expect that there is a negative association between career adaptability and COVID-19-related career worries and career uncertainty (H3). Assuming a potential mediating role of career adaptability, we expect that the effect of career preparation activities on career-related cognitions (career worries and uncertainty) is mediated via career adaptability (H4). In addition, in line with career construction theories, we assume that life satisfaction can be promoted by school-based career preparation activities (H5), that life satisfaction is positively associated with career adaptability (H6), and negatively with career worries and uncertainty (H7).

As indicated in Figure 1, we thus test for possible (a) direct effects of career preparation activities on career adaptability, career worries, and uncertainty as well as life satisfaction without mediation; (b) mediation via career adaptability; (c) mediation (including sequential mediation) via career worries and uncertainty; and (d) independent effects via career worries and uncertainty.

The model will control for a range of sociodemographic indicators which could have an effect on career construction processes and life satisfaction. In particular, we take into account the role of gender, age, ethnic minority status, past free school meal eligibility (an indicator of family socioeconomic status), and region. Although the evidence regarding these factors and the development of career adaptability is inconclusive, general assumptions are that there is a negative association between career adaptability and male gender, being younger, ethnic minority, and socially disadvantaged background (Hirschi, 2009; Patton & Creed, 2001). There is also evidence to suggest that there are regional differences in career preparedness (Hutchins & Akos, 2013).

Method

Participants and Data Collection

The study draws on longitudinal data from the first six waves of the Youth Economic Health Monitor (YEAH) survey, which were fielded between February 2021 and October 2022 (February—21, May—21, July—21, October—21, February—22, May—22). The YEAH survey is a quarterly quota panel study of 16–25-year-old UK residents recruited from web access panels managed by Ipsos Mori and partners. The survey collects information on mental health including life satisfaction alongside data on education, work, career readiness, skills development, and the perceived effects of COVID-19 on their lives. Given the lockdown restrictions and resource constraints, computer-assisted web interviewing was the only feasible data collection mode.

A quota sampling approach was chosen to recruit a balanced sample of a usually difficult to reach demographic during the second wave of the pandemic in the winter of 2021. For the initial sample, quotas were set according to age within gender, working status, and region. In conjunction with supplied survey weights, the sample was designed to be nationally representative. The survey sampled 1,000 young people in each wave. Follow-up samples were recruited among previous participants when possible and refreshed according to the quotas described above to make up for attrition when necessary. The longitudinal response rate was 62%.

Previous analysis showed that the YEAH sample was overall well balanced compared with other major data collections during the pandemic, such as the UK Household Longitudinal Study (UK-HLS) COVID-19 surveys and the Quarterly Labour Force Survey, the largest regular random probability household survey in the United Kingdom (Henseke et al., 2022). Table E1 in the Electronic Supplementary Material (ESM 1) compares key descriptive statistics from the YEAH study sample in comparison to UK-HLS and the Labour Force Survey. The study has received full ethical approval by the UCL IoE Research Ethics Committee and is registered with the UCL Data Protection Office (Z6364106/2020/10/90).

For the analysis, we restricted our sample to those with full information who participated in waves 2–6 (May 2021–May 2022) during each of which all core measures such as career adaptability or career worries were assessed. The analytic sample comprises $n = 4,040$ observations from $N = 2,673$ young people (52% female with an average age of $M_{age} = 20.95$ ($SD_{age} = 2.73$), of which 44.5% were in education, 47% were in work, and 8.5% were not in education, employment, or training). For more information, on the sample, see Tables E1 and E2 in ESM 1.

Measures

Participation in Career Preparation Activities was assessed with questions about a range of activities offered within schools and colleges: Some schools and colleges arrange for their students to participate in activities with employers or local business people. Have you done any of the following activities arranged by your school or college since you turned 14: internship or work experience; being mentored; enterprise competitions and challenges; careers advice; CV or interview workshops/practice; workplace visits or job shadowing; taking part in classroom discussions about job prospects or employment. Answers were coded as: (1) Yes, once; (2) Yes, more than once; (0) No, never, don't know, prefer not to say. Given the age range of our sample and their different activity states, we conducted robustness checks with a subsample of those who were aged 19+ or those below 19 and not in education ($n = 2,998$) to ensure the models estimate the relationship of past rather than concurrent school-based career preparation activities with career adaptability and the other measures.

Career Adaptability was measured with the 12 item Career Adapt–Abilities Scale–Short Form (CAAS-SF; Maggiori et al., 2017) which is strongly correlated with the widely used 24-item CAAS (Savickas & Porfeli, 2012). For the analysis, we focus on composite career adaptability aggregated across the four dimensions of concern (e.g., "thinking about what my future will be like"), control (e.g., "taking responsibility for my actions"), curiosity (e.g., "observing different ways of doing things"), and confidence (e.g., "solving problems"), which is a more reliable indicator and stronger predictor of relevant outcomes than individual components (Rudolph, Lavigne, & Zacher, 2017).

Career Uncertainty was measured with two items, asking students about the likelihood that they will have a job that pays well or a job that they enjoy doing ("Thinking about how you see your future, what are the chances that …?"). These two questions were adopted from the 10-item Perceived Life Chances Scale (Jessor et al., 1988) which has been established as a valid predictor of psychosocial adjustment of young adults (Hitlin & Johnson, 2015).

Career Worries were assessed with two questions: "To what extent, if at all, do you think your career prospects have been affected by the coronavirus pandemic? and "Overall, to what extent do you think your progress in learning job skills has been affected by the coronavirus pandemic?" Both questions were coded on the same response scale ranging from "Worsened a lot"/"worsened a little"/"remained the same as it would have done if there were no coronavirus pandemic"/"improved a little"/"improved a lot."

Life Satisfaction, the cognitive evaluation of one's life as a whole was assessed using a single item: "Overall, how satisfied are you with your life nowadays?" with responses options from 0 "Not at all satisfied" to 10 "Completely satisfied." The single-item question is used in many social surveys in the United Kingdom (ONS, 2018) and beyond (VanderWeele et al., 2020) and performs similarly to multi-item life satisfaction measures across various contexts (Cheung & Lucas, 2014).

Control Variables

The estimation models include a range of time-invariant sociodemographic control variables. These comprise age; gender; region of residence in the United Kingdom; parental level of education (differentiating parents with (1) secondary education or below, (2) upper-secondary level attainment as measured by A-levels or equivalent, and (3) those who achieved tertiary qualifications); receipt of free school meal during school years (a widely used indicator of childhood poverty; Day et al., 2016); as well as wave to control for variations in the measures over time.

Table 1. Measurement models: correlation between observed indicators and the latent variables (N = 4,040)

Latent variables and their indicators	Correlation coefficient	R^2
School-based career preparation		
Internship or work experience	.510	.260
Being mentored	.480	.231
Enterprise competition and challenges	.430	.185
Careers advice	.502	.252
CV or interview workshops/practice	.583	.340
Workplace visits or job shadowing	.547	.299
Taking part in classroom discussion about job prospects/employment	.486	.236
Career adaptability		
Concern (planning)	.736	.542
Control (self-determination)	.779	.597
Curiosity (career exploration)	.802	.644
Career self-confidence	.771	.594
Career uncertainty		
Will have a job that pays well (don't know)	.561	.315
Will have a job that you enjoy doing (don't know)	.801	.643
Career worries		
Job skill learning affected by the coronavirus pandemic	.679	.453
Career prospects have been affected by the coronavirus pandemic	.685	.469

Analytical Strategy

We use linear structural equation modeling (SEM) as implemented in STATA 17 in the pooled sample. SEM enables us to simultaneously estimate the structural relationships of school-based career preparation activities, career adaptation, career worries, and uncertainty and life satisfaction. Pooling the sample treats the data set as a cross-section to gain statistical power. This is appropriate because the hypotheses aim to establish longer-term relationships between school-based career preparation and later life outcomes. However, the sample includes repeated observations within individuals and is thus unlikely to meet the joint normality assumption of standard SEM. To adjust for potential autocorrelation within individuals over time in hypothesis tests, we compute standard errors clustered by panel members using the generalized Huber/White/sandwich estimator as implemented in STATA 17. Estimates use the supplied survey weights to correct potential sampling bias. Overall model fit is assessed using the coefficient of determination (R^2) and standardized root mean squared residual. Other commonly reported goodness-of-fit metrics such as the root mean square of approximation or the comparative fit index rely on the assumption of joint normality of the observed variables, which will be violated due to repeated observations for individuals in the pooled sample. This is an observational study and makes no causal assertions. Terms such as "effect" are used in a purely statistical sense.

Results

Table 1 shows the measurement models for the latent variables. All correlations coefficients between the predicted latent variable and the observed indicators were >.43 suggesting appropriate assessment. Figure 1 shows the structural model linking the focal variables providing standardized (β) path coefficients. The model has a good model fit (R^2 = 0.2, SRMR = .023: within the limit of 0.08).

The findings show that school-based career preparations are significantly and positively associated with career adaptability and life satisfaction and negatively with career uncertainty (see Figure 1). Career adaptability in turn is negatively associated with career worries and uncertainty and is positively associated with life satisfaction. In addition, we find negative associations between career worries and uncertainty and life satisfaction. The findings suggest sequential mediating processes, where the effect of school-based career preparation activities on career uncertainty and life satisfaction is partly mediated via career adaptability. In addition, we find a direct association between career adaptability and life satisfaction as well as mediation via career worries and uncertainties. Interestingly, there is no direct association between school-based career preparation and COVID-19-related career worries. Overall, the estimated directs effects

Table 2. Correlations between the endogenous and control variables (N = 4,040)

Control variables	Career preparation	Career adaptability	Career uncertainty	Career worries	Life satisfaction
Controls					
Age	−0.021	0.072**	−0.020	−0.186***	−0.092***
Female	−0.109***	0.035	0.018	0.059*	−0.099***
Ethnic minority	0.046	−0.024	0.032	0.028	−0.057***
High parental education	0.142***	0.072**	−0.012	0.078**	0.060**
Low parental education	−0.019	0.020	0.023	−0.005	−0.031
Free school meals	0.153***	0.004	0.001	−0.074**	−0.011
Region					
North & Yorkshire (REF)					
North West	−0.036	−0.022	0.017	−0.023	0.026
Midlands	−0.012	−0.001	−0.024	−0.001	−0.026
South West & Wales	0.005	0.035	0.011	0.006	0.000
South East & Anglia	0.000	0.020	−0.012	0.023	−0.020
Greater London	0.041	0.091**	0.011	−0.018	0.011
Scotland	−0.036	0.003	0.020	0.030	0.003
Northern Ireland	0.071	−0.008	0.003	−0.006	0.001
Wave					
3	−0.002	0.005	0.034	−0.004	0.045**
4	0.010	0.010	0.012	−0.091***	0.044*
5	0.047*	−0.014	0.000	−0.054*	0.042*
6	0.111***	−0.007	0.002	−0.091***	0.051**

Note. Estimated beta coefficients. Clustered standard errors to adjust for repeated observations within individuals. $*p < .05$. $**p < .01$. $***p < .001$.

between the endogenous variables tended to be small using common thresholds (small effect size = 0.1–0.29).

Inspecting the correlations between the endogenous and the control variables (Table 2) shows evidence of small sociodemographic variations in the endogenous variables. Older study members reported higher levels of career adaptability ($\beta = 0.07$) and fewer career worries ($\beta = -.19$) but lower levels of life satisfaction all else equal ($\beta = -.09$) than their younger peers. Women reported slightly lower levels of career preparations ($\beta = -0.1$), marginally greater career worries ($\beta = .06$), and lower levels of life satisfaction ($\beta = -0.1$) than men. Ethnic minority youth reported minimally lower levels of life satisfaction ($\beta = -0.06$) compared to White study members. Young people with higher educated parents tended to report higher levels of career preparation ($\beta = .14$), slightly greater career adaptability ($\beta = .07$), and life satisfaction ($\beta = .06$) as well as slightly elevated career worries ($\beta = .08$) than those with parents educated to upper-secondary levels. Those who were eligible for free school meals reported higher levels of career preparation activities ($\beta = .15$) and fewer career worries ($\beta = .08$) than those from better-off backgrounds. Regarding regional variations, we find that young people in London report higher levels of career adaptability than those in other regions.

There are also differences over time, with average career preparation increasing since February 22, career worries declining since May 2021, and life satisfaction increasing since July 2021, reflecting less stringent lockdown restrictions and economic recovery after the COVID-19 shock.

Running the models only for those age 19 years plus or those younger than 19 but no longer in education showed the same central results (i.e., similar effect sizes and patterns of statistical significance) as the ones reported in Figure 1, suggesting robustness of findings within different age subsamples.

Discussion

This study suggests that participation in school-based career preparation activities is directly associated with higher levels of career adaptability, lower career-related uncertainty, and higher life satisfaction. Using data from a survey of young people (YEAH survey) conducted in the aftermath of the initial COVID-19 shock, this is one of the first studies to assess the relevance of school-based career preparation activities in supporting career construction processes in the face of uncertainty and a changing education and employment landscape. We derived seven hypotheses within a sequential mediating model of career construction. The findings add to the debate regarding the malleability of career adaptability as postulated in career construction theories (Koen et al., 2012) and confirm key assumptions regarding the role of career adaptability resources in supporting effective career-related cognitions as well as life satisfaction (Savickas et al., 2009; Super et al., 1996). In addition, the findings provide new insights into the processes linking school-based career preparation activities to the career construction process and of young people.

The findings confirm the relationship of career adaptability with school-based career preparation activities (H1). Moreover, career adaptability resources are associated with effective career-related cognitions (reduced career worries and uncertainty) even in the face of a major economic upheaval (H2) and with higher levels of life satisfaction in young people (H6).

In addition, the findings provide support for the assumption that school-based career preparation activities can promote young people's career construction processes. We find that school-based career preparation activities are associated with more career adaptability resources (H1), lower career uncertainty (H2), and higher life satisfaction (H5). Notably, school-based career preparation activities are not significantly associated with COVID-19-related career worries, confirming assumption H2 only partially. Both career worries and uncertainty are however significantly associated with career adaptability (H3). The potential effect of school-based career preparation activities on career worries appears to be mediated via career adaptability (H4), while for career uncertainty this mediation is only partial. Potentially, school-based career preparation activities directly enable young people to develop specific longer-term career ambitions and a firm view about their future employment, but they cannot fully prepare young people to handle the short-term interruptions of changing education and employment opportunities due to the COVID-19 pandemic, unless through relevant career adaptability resources. Both career uncertainty and in particular career worries show a negative association with life satisfaction (H7), highlighting the relevant role of career-related cognitions in young people's lives. Notably, life satisfaction appears to be more affected by current career worries than longer-term career expectations, supporting assumptions that life satisfaction is strongly influenced by one's immediate situational context (Diener et al. 2018). For a comprehensive understanding of career construction processes, it is thus important to consider how individuals adjust to the challenges of a changing social context and to differentiate between short-term and longer-term strategies.

The findings confirm assumptions postulated within career construction theory, in particular regarding the role of career adaptability, as a relevant and learnable resource to support career-relevant attitudes and cognitions as well as life satisfaction (Savickas et al., 2009). In addition, the study provides new insights into the processes linking school-based career preparation activities with career-relevant attitudes and cognitions (Cedefop, 2021; Mann et al., 2020) as well as life satisfaction. In particular, the study tested sequential mediation processes linking school-based career preparation activities to career adaptability, career-related cognitions, and to life satisfaction. We find that school-based career preparation activities have a direct effect on career adaptability, career uncertainty, and life satisfaction, as described above. The direct effect of school-based career preparation activities on career uncertainty suggests that these activities address longer-term career decision-making processes (Hirschi & Laege, 2007; Perdrix et al., 2012), but there is no direct association with concurrent COVID-19-related career worries. Moreover, career adaptability partially mediates the influence of school-based career preparation activities on subsequent career-related cognitions and life satisfaction. Career uncertainty and career worries, in turn, independently mediate the association between career adaptability and life satisfaction. The findings thus indicate that school-based career preparation activities partly operate through career adaptability and career-related cognitions to influence life satisfaction.

The findings also suggest a direct association between school-based career preparation activities and life satisfaction. Taking into account the direct effect of school-based career preparation activities on career adaptability and career uncertainty, it can be assumed that the school-based career preparations contribute to subjective well-being by supporting the development of career adaptability (i.e., career planning and exploration, decision-making, and self-confidence), future career expectations and potentially also by establishing connections to employers and exposure to the labor market.

Regarding the influence of the control variables, the findings suggest that some facets of relative disadvantage (free school meal receipt, ethnic minority) predicted greater engagement in school-based career preparation activities. Future studies will have to show if these groups benefitted especially from the school-based career preparation activities regarding later employment outcomes. Interestingly, fewer women than men participated in school-based career preparation activities, potentially suggesting that the activities were more attractive to males. It could also be the case that women are generally more academically oriented (Schoon & Heckhausen, 2019). They also show slightly higher levels of career adaptability than males. The career preparation activities on offer might have been more targeted at skilled rather than professional jobs or jobs that women were less interested in. The findings also suggest that all things considered, those who are older expressed more COVID-19-related career worries, despite having higher levels of career adaptability than their younger peers. This finding thus only partly confirms the assumption that career decision-making difficulties decrease with age (Perdrix et al., 2012), highlighting the importance of contextual influences. Career adaptability might be higher, but COVID-19-related career worries are also high for those who are on the cusp of establishing themselves in the labor market compared to those who are still in education in the aftermath of a global pandemic. Future research needs to study these contextual influences in more detail. Interestingly, the study also found that those in Greater London show higher levels of career adaptability than those in other regions, possibly pointing to the importance of greater employment opportunities and exposure to different employment contexts in the capital city.

Strengths and Limitations

In interpreting the findings, a number of limitations have to be considered. The online study is largely based on self-reports not observed data. The sample is based only on those young people with access to the internet, limiting the generalization of findings to this group. Family SES was assessed based on reports of young people, which can introduce potential reporting bias. The relatively small sample limits the scope for subgroup analysis to test if the estimated relationships hold across different demographic groups. It would be worthwhile to examine differences in the pathways linking school-based career preparation activities to career construction processes among different subpopulations in more detail. It is conceivable that those from relative disadvantaged background (i.e., ethnic minority groups or those who are eligible for free school meals) benefit relatively more from the participation of these activities. Moreover, the short time dimension of the panel limits the analyses of potential associations between school-based career preparation activities and longer-term career development in the aftermath of the pandemic. We did not make full use of the longitudinal nature of the data, and future studies should examine intraindividual variations over time or potential reverse causalities in more detail. Finally, the nonrandom nature of the sample and focus on the UK hampers generalizability to other contexts. Despite these limitations, this study enables a more comprehensive understanding of the processes linking school-based career preparation activities to career construction processes and life satisfaction of young people during the COVID-19 pandemic. Indeed, a major strength of the study is the assessment of a wide range of school-based career preparation activities offered in collaboration with local employers and business and the focus on a current cohort of young people coming of age during a major health pandemic. Yet, the survey does not include information on the quality or exact content of the career preparation activities or the qualifications of the instructors, and future studies should examine these in more detail.

Conclusion

As suggested by the sequential mediating model of career construction, school-based career preparation activities offered in collaboration with local employers and business can support young people in the development of career adaptability resources and career-relevant cognitions. Career-related activities while studying can also contribute to higher levels of life satisfaction even in times of a major global pandemic. The findings highlight the crucial role of schools in preparing young people for the world of work. Ideally, career preparation activities should be done in collaboration with employers, facilitating social networks, exposure to real-life challenges and opportunities, and providing relevant skills of how to manage new social roles. Especially in times of economic upheaval and uncertainty, such as those encountered in the aftermath of the global COVID-19 pandemic, individuals have to increasingly rely on their own resources and networks. Creating the right conditions in the school context to prepare young people for this undertaking should not only be focused on specific tasks such as making career decisions but preparing young people for both predictable and unpredictable transitions and changes in their career paths ahead.

Electronic Supplementary Material

The electronic supplementary material is available with the online version of the article at https://doi.org/10.1027/2151-2604/a000530

ESM 1. Table E1: Comparison of key descriptive statistics. Table E2: Summary statistics of the observed exogenous and endogenous variables.

References

Akkermans, J., Paradnike, K., Van der Heijden, B., & De Vos, A. (2018). The best of both worlds: The role of career adaptability and career competencies in students' well-being and performance. *Frontiers in Psychology, 9*, Article 1678. https://doi.org/10.3389/fpsyg.2018.01678

Akkermans, J., Richardson, J., & Kraimer, M. L. (2020). The Covid-19 crisis as a career shock: Implications for careers and vocational behavior. *Journal of Vocational Behavior*, 119, Article 103434. https://doi.org/10.1016/j.jvb.2020.103434

Blustein, D. L. (1987). Integrating career counseling and psychotherapy—A comprehensive treatment strategy. *Psychotherapy*, 24(4), 794–799. https://doi.org/10.1037/h0085781

Camussi, E., Meneghetti, D., Sbarra, M. L., Rella, R., Grigis, P., & Annovazzi, C. (2023). What future are you talking about? Efficacy of Life Design Psy-Lab, as career guidance intervention, to support university students' needs during COVID-19 emergency. *Frontiers in Psychology*, 13, Article 1023738. https://doi.org/10.3389/fpsyg.2022.1023738

Cedefop (2021). *Investing in career guidance*. https://www.etf.europa.eu/en/publications-and-resources/publications/investing-career-guidance

Chen, H. R., Fang, T. T., Liu, F., Pang, L. M., Wen, Y., Chen, S., & Gu, X. Y. (2020). Career adaptability research: A literature review with scientific knowledge mapping in web of science. *International Journal of Environmental Research and Public Health*, 17(16), Article 5986. https://doi.org/10.3390/ijerph17165986

Cheung, F., & Lucas, R. E. (2014). Assessing the validity of single-item life satisfaction measures: Results from three large samples. *Quality of Life Research*, 23(10), 2809–2818. https://doi.org/10.1007/s11136-014-0726-4

Covacevich, C., Mann, A., Santos, C., & Champaud, J. (2021). *Indicators of teenage career readiness: An analysis of longitudinal data from eight countries*. OECD Education Working Papers, no. 258. https://doi.org/10.1787/cec854f8-en

Day, S. E., Hinterland, K., Myers, C., Gupta, L., Harris, T. G., & Konty, K. J. (2018). A school-level proxy measure for individual-level poverty using school-level eligibility for free and reduced-price meals. *Journal of School Health*, 86(3), 204–214. https://doi.org/10.1111/josh.12371

Diener, E., Oishi, S., & Tay, L. (2018). Advances in subjective well-being research. *Nature Human Behavior*, 2(4), 253–260. https://doi.org/10.1038/s41562-018-0307-6

Engzell, P., Frey, A., & Verhagen, M. D. (2021). Learning loss due to school closures during the COVID-19 pandemic. *Proceedings of the National Academy of Sciences*, 118(17), Article e2022376118. https://doi.org/10.1073/pnas.2022376118

Fiori, M., Bollmann, G., & Rossier, J. (2015). Exploring the path through which career adaptability increases job satisfaction and lowers job stress: The role of affect. *Journal of Vocational Behavior*, 91, 113–121. https://doi.org/10.1016/j.jvb.2015.08.010

Green, F., Henseke, G., & Schoon, I. (2022). Perceived effects of the Covid-19 pandemic on educational progress and the learning of job skills: New evidence on young adults in the United Kingdom. *Journal of Education and Work*, 35(5), 485–501. https://doi.org/10.1080/13639080.2022.20926

Green, Z. A., Noor, U., & Hashemi, M. N. (2020). Furthering proactivity and career adaptability among university students: Test of intervention. *Journal of Career Assessment*, 28(3), 402–424. https://doi.org/10.1177/1069072719870739

Griffin, B., & Hesketh, B. (2003). Adaptable behaviours for successful work and career adjustment. *Australian Journal of Psychology*, 55(2), 65–73. https://doi.org/10.1080/00049530412331312914

Hartung, P., & Cadaret, M. (2017). Career adaptability: Changing self and situation for satisfaction and success. In K. Maree (Ed.), *Psychology of career adaptability, employability and resilience* (pp. 15–28). Springer International Publishing.

Hartung, P. J., & Taber, B. J. (2008). Career construction and subjective well-being. *Journal of Career Assessment*, 16(1), 75–85. https://doi.org/10.1177/1069072707305772

Henehen, K. (2021). *Uneven steps. Changes in youth unemployment and study since the onset of Covid-19*. https://www.resolutionfoundation.org/publications/uneven-steps/

Henseke, G., Green, F., & Schoon, I. (2022). Living with COVID-19: Subjective well-being in the second phase of the pandemic. *Journal of Youth and Adolescence*, 51(9), 1679–1692. https://doi.org/10.1007/s10964-022-01648-8

Hirschi, A. (2009). Career adaptability development in adolescence: Multiple predictors and effect on sense of power and life satisfaction. *Journal of Vocational Behavior*, 74(2), 145–155. https://doi.org/10.1016/j.jvb.2009.01.002

Hirschi, A., Herrmann, A., & Keller, A. C. (2015). Career adaptivity, adaptability, and adapting: A conceptual and empirical investigation. *Journal of Vocational Behavior*, 87, 1–10. https://doi.org/10.1016/j.jvb.2014.11.008

Hirschi, A., & Koen, J. (2021). Contemporary career orientations and career self-management: A review and integration. *Journal of Vocational Behavior*, 126, Article 103505. https://doi.org/10.1016/j.jvb.2020.103505

Hirschi, A., & Laege, D. (2007). The relation of secondary students' career-choice readiness to a six-phase model of career decision making. *Journal of Career Development*, 34(2), 164–191. https://doi.org/10.1177/0894845307307473

Hirschi, A., & Lage, D. (2008). Using accuracy of self-estimated interest type as a sign of career choice readiness in career assessment of secondary students. *Journal of Career Assessment*, 16(3), 310–325. https://doi.org/10.1177/1069072708317372

Hitlin, S., & Johnson, M. K. (2015). Reconceptualizing agency within the life course: The power of looking ahead. *American Journal of Sociology*, 120(5), 1429–1472. https://doi.org/10.1086/681216

Hutchins, B. C., & Akos, P. (2013). Rural high school youth's access to and use of school-to-work programs. *Career Development Quarterly*, 61(3), 210–225. https://doi.org/10.1002/j.2161-0045.2013.00050.x

Jessor, R., Donovan, J. E., & Costa, F. (1988). *Denver Health Behavior Questionnaire Boulder*. Institute of Behavioral Science, University of Colorado.

Johnston, C. S. (2018). A systematic review of the career adaptability literature and future outlook. *Journal of Career Assessment*, 26(1), 3–30. https://doi.org/10.1177/1069072716679921

Khalid, K., & Ahmad, A. M. (2021). The relationship between employability skills and career adaptability: A case of undergraduate students of the United Arab Emirates. *Higher Education Skills and Work-Based Learning*, 11(5), 1035–1054. https://doi.org/10.1108/heswbl-08-2020-0175

Koen, J., Klehe, U.-C., & Van Vianen, A. E. M. (2012). Training career adaptability to facilitate a successful school-to-work transition. *Journal of Vocational Behavior*, 81(3), 395–408. https://doi.org/10.1016/j.jvb.2012.10.003

Lent, R. W. (2013). Career-life preparedness: Revisiting career planning and adjustment in the new workplace. *Career Development Quarterly*, 61(1), 2–14. https://doi.org/10.1002/j.2161-0045.2013.00031.x

Lent, R. W., & Brown, S. D. (2013). Social cognitive model of career self-management: Toward a unifying view of adaptive career behavior across the life span. *Journal of Counseling Psychology*, 60(4), 557–568. https://doi.org/10.1037/a0033446

Lent, R. W., & Brown, S. D. (2019). Social cognitive career theory at 25: Empirical status of the interest, choice, and performance models. *Journal of Vocational Behavior*, 115, Article 103316. https://doi.org/10.1016/j.jvb.2019.06.004

Maggiori, C., Rossier, J., & Savickas, M. L. (2017). Career Adapt-Abilities Scale-Short Form (CAAS-SF): Construction and validation. *Journal of Career Assessment*, 25(2), 312–325. https://doi.org/10.1177/1069072714565856

Mann, A., Denis, V., & Percy, C. (2020). *Career ready? How schools can better prepare young people for working life in the era of Covid-19*. OECD Education Working Paper no 241. https://doi.org/10.1787/e1503534-en

Marciniak, J., Johnston, C. S., Steiner, R. S., & Hirschi, A. (2022). Career preparedness among adolescents: A review of key components and directions for future research. *Journal of Career Development, 49*(1), 18–40. https://doi.org/10.1177/0894845320943951

ONS. (2023). Measures of National Well-being Dashboard: Quality of Life in the UK. https://www.ons.gov.uk/peoplepopulationandcommunity/wellbeing/articles/measuresofnationalwellbeingdashboardqualityoflifeintheuk/2022-08-12

Pajic, S., Keszler, A., Kismihok, G., Mol, S. T., & Den Hartog, D. N. (2018). Antecedents and outcomes of Hungarian nurses' career adaptability. *International Journal of Manpower, 39*(8), 1096–1114. https://doi.org/10.1108/ijm-10-2018-0334

Patton, W., & Creed, P. A. (2001). Developmental issues in career maturity and career decision status. *Career Development Quarterly, 49*(4), 336–351. https://doi.org/10.1002/j.2161-0045.2001.tb00961.x

Perdrix, S., Stauffer, S., Masdonati, J., Massoudi, K., & Rossier, J. (2012). Effectiveness of career counseling: A one-year follow-up. *Journal of Vocational Behavior, 80*(2), 565–578. https://doi.org/10.1016/j.jvb.2011.08.011

Phillips, S. D., & Blustein, D. L. (1994). Readiness for career choices: Planning, exploring, and deciding. *The Career Development Quarterly, 43*(1), 63–73. https://doi.org/10.1002/j.2161-0045.1994.tb00847.x

Robertson, P. J. (2013). The well-being outcomes of career guidance. *British Journal of Guidance & Counselling, 41*(3), 254–266. https://doi.org/10.1080/03069885.2013.773959

Rudolph, C. W., Allan, B., Clark, M., Hertel, G., Hirschi, A., Kunze, F., Shockley, K., Shoss, M., Sonnentag, S., & Zacher, H. (2021). Pandemics: Implications for research and practice in industrial and organizational psychology. *Industrial and Organizational Psychology-Perspectives on Science and Practice, 14*(1-2), 1–35. https://doi.org/10.1017/iop.2020.48

Rudolph, C. W., Lavigne, K. N., Katz, I. M., & Zacher, H. (2017). Linking dimensions of career adaptability to adaptation results: A meta-analysis. *Journal of Vocational Behavior, 102*, 151–173. https://doi.org/10.1016/j.jvb.2017.06.003

Rudolph, C. W., Lavigne, K. N., & Zacher, H. (2017). Career adaptability: A meta-analysis of relationships with measures of adaptivity, adapting responses, and adaptation results. *Journal of Vocational Behavior, 98*, 17–34. https://doi.org/10.1016/j.jvb.2016.09.002

Santilli, S., Grossen, S., & Nota, L. (2020). Career adaptability, resilience, and fife satisfaction among Italian and Belgian middle school students. *Career Development Quarterly, 68*(3), 194–207. https://doi.org/10.1002/cdq.12231

Santilli, S., Marcionetti, J., Rochat, S., Rossier, J., & Nota, L. (2017). Career adaptability, hope, optimism, and life satisfaction in Italian and Swiss adolescents. *Journal of Career Development, 44*(1), 62–76. https://doi.org/10.1177/0894845316633793

Savickas, M. L. (1997). Career adaptability: An integrative construct for life-span, life-space theory. *Career Development Quarterly, 45*(3), 247–259. https://doi.org/10.1002/j.2161-0045.1997.tb00469.x

Savickas, M. L. (2005). The theory and practice of career construction. In S. D. Brown, & R. W. Lent (Eds.), *Career development and counseling: Putting theory and research to work* (pp. 42–70). Wiley.

Savickas, M. L. (2012). Life design: A paradigm for career intervention in the 21st century. *Journal of Counseling and Development, 90*(1), 13–19. https://doi.org/10.1111/j.1556-6676.2012.00002.x

Savickas, M. L., Nota, L., Rossier, J., Dauwalder, J. P., Duarte, M. E., Guichard, J., Soresi, S., Van Esbroeck, R., & van Vianen, A. E. M. (2009). Life designing: A paradigm for career construction in the 21st century. *Journal of Vocational Behavior, 75*(3), 239–250. https://doi.org/10.1016/j.jvb.2009.04.004

Savickas, M. L., & Porfeli, E. J. (2012). Career Adapt-Abilities Scale: Construction, reliability, and measurement equivalence across 13 countries. *Journal of Vocational Behavior, 80*(3), 661–673. https://doi.org/10.1016/j.jvb.2012.01.011

Schoon, I., & Bynner, J. (2019). Young people and the Great Recession: Variations in the school-to-work transition in Europe and the United States. *Longitudinal and Life Course Studies, 10*(2), 153–173. https://doi.org/10.1332/175795919X15514456677349

Schoon, I., & Heckhausen, J. (2019). Conceptualizing individual agency in the transition from school to work: A socio-ecological developmental perspective. *Adolescent Research Review, 4*(4), 135–148. https://doi.org/10.1007/s40894-019-00111-3

Spur, D., Kauffeld, S., Barthauer, L., & Heinemann, N. S. R. (2015). Fostering networking behavior, career planning and optimism, and subjective career success: An intervention study. *Journal of Vocational Behavior, 87*, 134–144. https://doi.org/10.1016/j.jvb.2014.12.007

Super, D. E. (1957). *The psychology of careers*. Harper & Row.

Super, D. E. (1980). A life-span, life-space approach to career development. *Journal of Vocational Behavior, 16*(3), 282–298. https://doi.org/10.1016/0001-8791(8090056-1)

Super, D. E. (1993). The 2 faces of counseling—Or is it 3. *Career Development Quarterly, 42*(2), 132–136. https://doi.org/10.1002/j.2161-0045.1993.tb00425.x

Super, D. E., Savickas, M. L., & Super, C. M. (1996). The life-span, life-space approach to careers. In D. Brown, & B. L. (Eds.), *Career Choice and development: Applying contemporary theories to practice* (3rd ed., pp. 121–178). Jossey-Bass.

Taber, B. J., & Blankemeyer, M. (2015). Future work self and career adaptability in the prediction of proactive career behaviors. *Journal of Vocational Behavior, 86*, 20–27. https://doi.org/10.1016/j.jvb.2014.10.005

VanderWeele, T. J., Trudel-Fitzgerald, C., Allin, P., Farrelly, C., Fletcher, G., Frederick, D. E., Hall, J., Helliwell, J. F., Kim, E. S., Lauinger, W. A., Lee, M. T., Lyubomirsky, S., Margolis, S., McNeely, E., Messer, N., Tay, L., Viswanath, V., Węziak-Białowolska, D., & Kubzansky, L. D. (2020). Current recommendations on the selection of measures for well-being. *Preventive Medicine, 133*, Article 106004. https://doi.org/10.1016/j.ypmed.2020.106004

Verbruggen, M., & Sels, L. (2008). Can career self-directedness be improved through counseling? *Journal of Vocational Behavior, 73*(2), 318–327. https://doi.org/10.1016/j.jvb.2008.07.001

Zacher, H. (2014). Career adaptability predicts subjective career success above and beyond personality traits and core self-evaluations. *Journal of Vocational Behavior, 84*(1), 21–30. https://doi.org/10.1016/j.jvb.2013.10.002

History

Received December 7, 2022
Revision received March 17, 2023
Accepted March 18, 2023
Published online July 18, 2023

Publication Ethics

The study has received full ethical approval by the UCL IoE Research Ethics Committee and is registered with the UCL Data Protection Office (Z6364106/2020/10/90).

ORCID

Ingrid Schoon
https://orcid.org/0000-0002-4262-3711

Golo Henseke
https://orcid.org/0000-0003-0669-2100

Ingrid Schoon

Social Research Institute
Institute of Education (IoE)
University College London (UCL)
55-59 Gordon Square
London WC1H 0AL
United Kingdom
i.schoon@ucl.ac.uk

Original Article

The Role of Basic Need Satisfaction for Motivation and Self-Regulated Learning During COVID-19

A Longitudinal Study

Elisabeth Rosa Pelikan[1], Luisa Grützmacher[2], Katharina Hager[1], Julia Holzer[1], Selma Korlat[1], Martin Mayerhofer[3], Barbara Schober[1], Christiane Spiel[1], and Marko Lüftenegger[1,2]

[1]Department of Developmental and Educational Psychology, Faculty of Psychology, University of Vienna, Austria
[2]Department of Teacher Education, Center for Teacher Education, University of Vienna, Austria
[3]Department of Mathematics, Faculty of Mathematics, University of Vienna, Austria

Abstract: Higher education institutions in Austria switched to emergency distance learning in March 2020 to mitigate the spread of COVID-19. Due to the sudden change, students and instructors scarcely had time to adjust to the new demands. Initial cross-sectional studies pointed to the risks of emergency distance learning for students' intrinsic motivation, self-regulation, and learning behavior. We investigated the longitudinal effects between the satisfaction of the basic psychological needs (competence, autonomy, and social relatedness), intrinsic motivation, and self-regulated learning, applying a cross-lagged panel model. A sample of $N = 3,286$ students answered four online questionnaires between April 2020 and July 2021. All measured constructs remained stable during that time span. The satisfaction of the basic needs was cross-sectionally related to intrinsic motivation. We found no cross-lagged effects on intrinsic motivation. Self-regulated learning showed small but significant cross-lagged positive effects on intrinsic motivation at all time points. Implications and future research perspectives are discussed.

Keywords: self-determination theory, basic need satisfaction, self-regulated learning, COVID-19, higher education

Higher education changed dramatically due to COVID-19 and the subsequent measures to mitigate the spread of the virus. In Austria, all educational institutions were switched to emergency distance learning in March 2020 and continued to be so for over a year. The closure of all universities in Austria marked a significant change in its higher education landscape, where classes had, until then, been largely conducted face-to-face. Moreover, due to the sudden switch, students and instructors had little time to adjust to the demands of the new learning situation. Initial cross-sectional studies pointed to the risks of emergency distance learning for students' learning motivation, self-regulation, and learning behavior (e.g., Hensley et al., 2022; Holzer et al., 2021), which is particularly concerning, as both intrinsic motivation (e.g., Jeno et al., 2023) and self-regulated learning (e.g., Broadbent & Poon, 2015) are considered foundational for successful learning and academic success.

Self-determination theory (SDT; Ryan & Deci, 2020) is a psychological theory that emphasizes the importance of autonomy, competence, and social relatedness for human growth and motivation and provides an important framework for understanding intrinsic motivation (e.g., Mukhtar et al., 2018) and resilience (e.g., Carmona-Halty et al., 2019; Trigueros et al., 2019) in the face of adversity. SDT claims to be universal and applicable in different contexts and across different cultures (Ryan & Deci, 2020). However, it also highlights the importance of a supportive social environment for need satisfaction (Ryan & Deci, 2020). Thus, a fundamental change such as the sudden shift to emergency distance learning during COVID-19 is likely to affect basic need satisfaction (Bartholomew et al., 2011). In addition, while face-to-face teaching provides a certain amount of structure, distance learning offers more autonomy for students but also requires them to self-regulate their learning to a higher degree to keep up with their studies (Klingsieck et al., 2012).

Although the relation between basic need satisfaction and intrinsic motivation as well as the importance of self-regulated learning for online learning has been studied before, longitudinal studies examining these constructs together are scarce and – to our knowledge – nonexistent in the context of emergency distance learning during COVID-19. However, knowledge about their interaction during COVID-19 may provide important insights for how educational systems can prepare for future health and related economic crises to mitigate the impact on student learning and psychosocial functioning.

In the present study, we therefore investigate the interplay of the satisfaction of the three basic psychological needs, intrinsic motivation, and self-regulated learning during the extended closures of higher education institutions in Austria, with the aim of gathering insights on how best to support students in distance learning and possible future crises situations.

Basic Psychological Need Satisfaction as Foundation for Intrinsic Motivation

SDT (Ryan & Deci, 2020) assumes that the satisfaction of the needs for perceived competence (feeling capable and self-effective in dealing with the demands of the environment), autonomy (feeling able to determine one's own actions), and social relatedness (having a sense of belonging and feeling as part of a group) is fundamental for optimal human functioning and a prerequisite for intrinsic motivation. Intrinsic motivation – engaging in activities based on interest and pleasure without extrinsic consequences – is considered the most self-determined type of motivation and the prototype for autonomous behavior (Ryan & Deci, 2020). The positive relationship between basic need satisfaction and intrinsic motivation, as proposed by SDT, has been confirmed in numerous studies in different domains (e.g., Ntoumanis et al., 2021; Rodrigues et al., 2021; Van den Broeck et al., 2016). In the educational context, previous research has shown that teaching styles that satisfy students' basic psychological needs lead to higher intrinsic motivation (e.g., Bureau et al., 2021). In turn, higher intrinsic motivation is associated with positive educational outcomes such as lower dropout rates (Jeno et al., 2023), higher persistence and engagement (Karimi & Sotoodeh, 2020), more effective study methods (Kusurkar et al., 2013), higher achievement (Hsu et al., 2019; Jeno et al., 2023), and better well-being (Jeno et al., 2023). Considering that distance learning provides less structure and social support to compensate for a potential lack of intrinsic motivation, it is deemed to be equally, if not more, important in distance learning settings than in regular face-to-face education (Hensley et al., 2022; Hsu et al., 2019).

Longitudinal studies on the stability and directional links between basic psychological need satisfaction and intrinsic motivation are still rare and have yielded mixed results. For example, Pan and Gauvain (2012) found a decline of autonomous motivation over the first two years in college although peer relatedness increased and parental autonomy support remained stable. This was supported by Corpus and colleagues (2020) who described a decrease in students' intrinsic motivation during the first year in college. In contrast, Müller and Palekčić (2005) report that students' need satisfaction and intrinsic learning motivation remained relatively stable over a period of three years, while perceived autonomy support and competence declined. Noyens and colleagues (2019) investigated the reciprocal relation of social integration and intrinsic motivation in first-year university students. In their study, students with higher social integration were more intrinsically motivated at the end of the year, whereas students who expressed no motivation had trouble finding social connections at university. These findings suggest that students' perceived competence and social integration may influence their self-regulation, which is in turn crucial for intrinsic motivation.

Self-Regulated Learning and Intrinsic Motivation

Another important aspect in less-structured learning settings is students' ability to self-regulate their learning. Strategies for self-regulated learning include planning and managing tasks and time; knowing, implementing, and adapting learning strategies; monitoring progress; seeking support if necessary; and reflecting upon successful and unsuccessful strategy use (Zimmerman, 2000). Various studies have pointed to the importance of self-regulated learning for online and distance learning. For example, in their meta-analysis, Broadbent and Poon (2015) found that time management, effort regulation, critical thinking, and metacognitive strategy use had a small but significant effect on academic achievement in online learning. Similarly, goal setting and strategic planning positively predicted goal attainment in free online courses (Kizilcec et al., 2017).

Regarding self-regulated learning, it would be reasonable to assume that students experience an increase in self-regulated learning competence during their studies. Accordingly, Higgins and colleagues (2021) report that after a decrease in the first year, students' self-regulated learning strategy use increased during the following two years at university. This echoes the findings of Ning and Downing (2010), who found that self-regulated learning strategy use increased within the first 15 months of university and that self-regulated learning predicted affective regulation (termed motivation by the authors). However, these findings somewhat contradict other studies, in which intrinsic motivation has been found to be a precursor to self-regulated learning strategy use. For example, Mukhtar and colleagues (2018) found that medical interns' willingness to self-regulate their learning was predicted by intrinsic motivation. Thus, it is not clear from the current state of research whether self-regulated learning changes over time, whether intrinsic motivation influences self-regulated learning or vice versa, or if there are bidirectional effects.

Basic Psychological Need Satisfaction and Self-Regulated Learning During Emergency Distance Learning During COVID-19

Beyond the requirements of regular distance learning, the rapid transition to emergency distance learning was accompanied by additional challenges and potential risks for basic psychological need satisfaction and self-regulated learning (Bozkurt et al., 2020; Janke et al., 2022). In the early days of distance learning in Austria, courses were often postponed and lectures were held asynchronously so that social interaction during lectures was very limited. Additionally, not only contact with fellow students and instructors were limited, but all social contact – be it inside or outside of university life – was restricted. It can be assumed that the satisfaction of the need for social relatedness was particularly compromised during this time.

Moreover, while distance learning is mostly actively chosen to take advantage of its benefits such as flexibility in time and place and compatibility with work or care obligations, the COVID-19 crisis forced all students into this form of learning, possibly thwarting the satisfaction of students' need for autonomy. Thus, while the higher autonomy of distance learning should theoretically lead to increased intrinsic motivation, the forced nature of emergency distance learning may have mitigated this (Hensley et al., 2022). It is also likely that there has been little or no structural support for distance learning established at most institutions (Campbell et al., 2022; Farnell et al., 2021). This is even more noteworthy as Ryan and Deci (2020) point out that a high level of autonomy should not be equated with a lack of structure and that autonomy is only beneficial if adequate competencies (e.g., for self-regulated learning) are in place to manage it successfully. However, the sudden switch to emergency distance learning left students hardly any time to adequately prepare for and instructors had almost no time to adapt the course material to the new setting and to acquire the corresponding didactic knowledge (Bozkurt et al., 2020; Farnell et al., 2021). Thus, it may have been even more relevant for students to apply self-regulated learning strategies to enhance their perceived competence and support their intrinsic motivation. This may have been particularly challenging, as the measures also restricted students' flexibility and options in choosing self-regulated learning strategies. For example, students reported that being confined to their homes deprived them of the opportunity to control their learning environment so that they had to study in a more distracting and disrupted setting than usual (Hensley et al., 2022). According to Zhang and colleagues (2021), the shift to online learning also changed students' planning and goal setting in such a way that they minimized their time and effort rather than opting for more intense learning strategies. Students cutting back on the use of self-regulated learning is alarming, especially since studies have found that students with high self-regulated learning strategy use coped better with the challenging situation of distance learning during COVID-19 and that interventions that promoted self-regulated learning turned out to be effective buffers against pandemic-related stressors (Hadwin et al., 2022). Considering these limiting factors, it is not clear whether basic psychological needs were adequately met during this period. Furthermore, the duration and intensity of the challenging situation – in this case, distance learning during COVID-19 – need to be considered when investigating the influence of basic need satisfaction as SDT implies that, while a lack of need satisfaction over a short period of time may be detrimental for students' intrinsic motivation and learning behavior, a long-term dissatisfaction of psychological needs has even worse consequences for motivation and mental health (Ryan et al., 2019). For example, it is possible that social relationships were still maintained at the beginning of the pandemic, but that the long duration of the restrictions and the effort it took to keep up contact had an increasingly negative impact on social relatedness.

Additionally, the unpredictable nature of COVID-19 has placed significant stress on students. For instance, while the closures of higher education institutions were initially expected to last only a few weeks, they eventually lasted more than a year. This forced both, students and teachers, to adapt to the long-term shift toward remote learning. In addition to disrupting everyday university life, new procedures to assess student learning had to be adapted, which caused additional stress and uncertainty among students. Overall, it can be concluded that the unanticipated and prolonged closures had either a delayed and/or sloping effect, particularly in terms of their basic psychological need satisfaction, motivation, and self-regulation.

The Present Study

Thus, the present study aims to examine the longitudinal directional effects between students' basic need satisfaction, intrinsic motivation, and self-regulated learning during emergency distance learning during COVID-19. Based on the literature reviewed, we hypothesize that the satisfaction of the three basic needs (perceived competence, autonomy, and social relatedness) is positively related to intrinsic motivation at each time point (H1). We are furthermore interested in the directional, cross-lagged effects of the three basic psychological needs on intrinsic motivation. In line with SDT, we hypothesize that perceived competence (H2a: T1 → T2, H2b: T2 → T3), autonomy (H2c: T1 → T2, H2d: T2 → T3), and social relatedness (H2e: T1 → T2, H2f: T2 → T3) are predicting intrinsic motivation at the next time point while controlling for all other paths. Finally, as students had to rely more on their own ability to organize and structure their learning due to the sudden switch to emergency distance learning and previous research failed to establish a clear directional effect, we want to explore the cross-sectional, longitudinal, and reciprocal links between self-regulated learning and intrinsic motivation. For an overview over our computed cross-lagged panel model, see Figure S1 in the Supplementary Material.

Method

Sample, Procedure, and Context of Data Collection

This study was undertaken as part of a larger study, in which Austrian students were asked about their learning and well-being during COVID-19. Initially, three waves of data collection were planned and executed: April 7–April 24, 2020 (T1), April 27–May 12, 2020 (T2), and June 8–June 29, 2020 (T3). In Austria, the first confirmed case of COVID-19 was reported on February 25, 2020. On March 16, 2020, all schools and universities were officially closed and a comprehensive curfew was imposed. While retail and museums were gradually reopened during April and May, universities remained closed, and classes were held exclusively through distance learning. Due to another surge of infections, hard lockdowns took place between November 17, 2020, and December 6, 2020; between December 26, 2021, and February 7, 2021; and between November 22, 2021, and December 11, 2021. Universities only reopened during the winter semester of 2021/2022 under continued protective measures (mandatory use of FFP2 masks, physical distancing, partially occupied lecture halls). Even then, educators were instructed to plan their classes in such a way that a switch to hybrid or online teaching would be possible at any time. For this reason, many classes were held online from the onset. Thus, a fourth measurement point was conducted from June 21st to July 31st, 2021 (T4), to gather data on the impact of the continuous distance learning of higher education students. Data from the first measurement point have been used in three prior publications (Holzer et al., 2021; Pelikan et al., 2021, 2022), although with different research questions and data analysis methods applied.

The link to the first online survey (T1) was distributed by various stakeholders (e.g., university rectorates and higher educational networks) and media outlets. The Austrian Federal Ministry of Education, Science, and Research recommended participation on their website. Prior to data collection, participants were informed about the study's goals and inclusion criteria (attending a higher education institution in Austria). Participation was voluntary. At the end of the first survey, students were invited to participate in the longitudinal study. If they approved, they were contacted via e-mail for subsequent measurement points. Only data from students who gave active consent were included in the data set. Data analysis was conducted with anonymized data. Comprehensive information about the project, the data cleaning process, and the full questionnaire for the first three measurement points can be found at the Austrian Social Science Data Archive (Schober et al., 2021). As the fourth measurement point was not part of the funded project, data are provided separately and can be accessed in the Open Science Framework (OSF) at https://www.doi.org/10.17605/OSF.IO/KX4WU (Pelikan et al., 2023). Overall, $N = 3,286$ students (72.0% female, 27.1% male, 0.4% diverse, 0.5% missing) with an average age of $M_{age} = 25.06$ ($SD_{age} = 7.038$, range = 14–71) consented to participate in the longitudinal study. Among the surveyed participants, a majority of 67.3% aimed to obtain a bachelor's degree, while 20.3% aspired for a master's degree. Attendance in a diploma program was reported by 10.1% of the respondents, with a further 0.5% attending a university course. Additionally, 1.3% of the respondents were enrolled in a doctoral program, while 0.5% did not provide any information.

Measures

The examined variables were part of an extensive online questionnaire that consisted of existing scales (adapted to the pandemic context) and a small number of newly developed items. All questions were answered on a rating scale of 1 (*strongly agree*) to 5 (*strongly disagree*) and recoded so that higher values indicate higher agreement. Students were instructed to relate their responses to the current situation (distance learning during COVID-19). To assess scale reliability, we first computed a confirmatory factor analysis incorporating all scales at all time points. The model attained an acceptable model fit [$\chi^2(1,919) = 4,347.171$, $p < .001$, RMSEA = .020 [.019, .020], CFI = .961, TLI = .954, SRMR = .052]. All factor loadings were >.30. Additionally, we computed the coefficient α (Cronbach & Shavelson, 2004) and measurement invariance (see Table S1 in the Supplementary Material for descriptive statistics and reliabilities for all scales at each time point and Table S2 for the results of the measurement invariance analysis).

Perceived autonomy was assessed with two newly developed items (e.g., "Currently, I can define my own areas of focus in my studies"; α = .739–.769 across measurement points).

Perceived competence was measured with three items based on the Work-related Basic Need Satisfaction Scale (W-BNS; Van den Broeck et al., 2016) and applied to the learning context (e.g., "Currently, I am dealing well with the demands of my studies"; α = .798–.824).

Perceived social relatedness was measured with three items. Two items were adapted from the W-BNS (Van den Broeck et al., 2016; e.g., "Currently, I feel connected with my fellow students"), whereas one item was based on the German Basic Psychological Need Satisfaction and Frustration Scale (Heissel et al., 2018; e.g., "Currently, I feel connected with the people who are important to me (family, friends)"; α = .686–.747).

Intrinsic motivation was assessed with three items based on the Scales for the Measurement of Motivational Regulation for Learning in University Students (SMR-LS; Thomas et al., 2018; e.g., "Currently, doing work for university is really fun"; α = .910–.922).

Self-regulated learning was assessed with five items based on the short version of the Learning strategies in study scale (Lernstrategien im Studium Kurzskala; LIST-K; Klingsieck, 2018; e.g., "In the current home-learning situation, I use different learning and working strategies") and one newly developed item ("In the current home-learning situation, I try to motivate myself (e.g., through rewards for each completed task)"; α = .704–.774)."

Data Analysis

Descriptive and missing data analyses were carried out using IBM SPSS version 27.0, whereas the longitudinal measurement invariance and the cross-lagged panel model (CLPM) were tested using Mplus version 8.6. To confirm the missing completely at random assumption, Little's MCAR test was applied (Little, 1988), $\chi^2(5,924) = 6,091.710, p = .063$. Missing data were handled by using the full information maximum likelihood method (Lüdtke et al., 2007). In all analyses performed in Mplus, we applied robust maximum likelihood estimators, as they offer the advantage of being robust against non-normally distributed data by correcting standard errors and the χ^2 distribution in the models (Satorra & Bentler, 1994). Goodness of fit was assessed by consulting CFI and TLI, considering cutoff values of >.95 and >.90 as excellent and adequate fit, respectively. Furthermore, RMSEA and SRMR with RMSEA < .06 and < .08. and SRMR < .11 and < .08 as cutoffs for excellent and adequate fit, respectively, were applied (Hu & Bentler, 1999). All tests for statistical significance were performed at the .05 level. However, due to the large sample, we did not rely on statistical significance when interpreting the results but additionally focused on the effect sizes, following Gignac and Szodorai (2016), according to which standardized values of .10, .20, and .30 reflect small, moderate, and large effect sizes, respectively.

Preliminary Analysis: Measurement Invariance Analysis

Before conducting the main analysis, we tested for measurement invariance across time points. The degree of measurement invariance determines the interpretation of the results in the following way: *Configural variance* across measurement points indicates that the item-to-construct relations are expected to be always at the same level. *Metric variance* determines whether the same meaning is attributed to the construct at all time points. At the highest level, *scalar invariance* establishes that the latent constructs are given the same meaning and the latent variable can be compared across all time points (Brown, 2015; Little et al., 2007). When this level of measurement invariance cannot be established, it is possible to test for partial scalar measurement invariance by setting single intercepts free, as some intercepts can be invariant, but not all of them (Brown, 2015). To investigate measurement invariance, we conducted confirmatory factor analyses (CFA) over time for each scale. In addition to the model fit criteria described above, changes in RMSEA and CFI were used to determine the level of invariance with a change of ΔRMSEA < .03, ΔCFI < − .02 and a change of ΔRMSEA < .01, ΔCFI < − .01, indicating metric and scalar invariance, respectively (Rutkowski & Svetina, 2014).

Main Analysis: Cross-Lagged Panel Model

To investigate the research questions, we conducted an autoregressive cross-lagged structural equation model in Mplus. The model can be used to examine the extent of stability or change of interindividual differences over time and to explain the change by other variables included in the model. As described above, data were initially collected at three time points during spring and early summer of 2020, with a fourth measurement point added in early summer 2021. To account for this procedure, we created the model in two steps. First, only the first three data collection time points were considered. Then, the model was extended to include the fourth measurement time point.

Results

Preliminary Analysis

Descriptive Statistics and Measurement Invariance

Descriptive statistics at each time point are reported in Table S1 in the Supplementary Material. Configural and metric but not scalar measurement could be established for all scales. Following Brown (2015), partial scalar measurement invariance could be established by freeing intercepts for all scales apart from intrinsic motivation (see Table S2 in the Supplementary Material section), where ΔRMSEA was slightly over the cutoff value. However, as Chen (2007) suggested a change of ≤.015 in RMSEA as sufficiently small and ΔCFI was well below the cutoff, we considered the model fit acceptable.

Cross-Sectional Correlations Between the Constructs

Pearson's correlations between all constructs at each time point are reported in Table 1. Perceived competence, autonomy, and social relatedness were positively associated with intrinsic motivation at all measurement points ($r = .232$ to $r = .641$). Moreover, all basic psychological needs and intrinsic motivation were positively related to self-regulated learning at all time points, albeit with small to moderate effect sizes ($r = .091$ to $r = .220$).

Main Analysis: Cross-Lagged Panel Model

The first model, including only the first three measurement points, fits the data well, $\chi^2(1,089) = 3,157.741$, $p < .001$; CFI = .962; TLI = .955; RMSEA = .024 [.023, .025]; SRMR = .053. Unstandardized and standardized effects of this model are presented in Table S3 and S4 in the Supplementary Material. However, since the cross-lagged panel model including all four measurement points fitted the data equally good, $\chi^2(1,994) = 4,550.637$, $p < .001$; CFI = .959; TLI = .953; RMSEA = .020 [.019, .021]; SRMR = .055, we decided to rely on this model to answer the research questions, for reasons of parsimony. Unstandardized and standardized effects of the residual correlations at each time point are presented in Table S5, and unstandardized and standardized effects of the autoregressive and cross-lagged effects are reported in Tables S6 and S7 in the Supplementary Material.

Stability of Basic Psychological Needs, Intrinsic Motivation, and Self-Regulated Learning

In a cross-lagged panel model, autoregressive effects represent the stability of individual differences in the constructs from one measurement point to the next. A large autoregressive coefficient means that "individual's relative standings on the construct has changed very little over time" (Selig & Little, 2012, p. 266). In our model, all autoregressive effects were significant ($p = <.001$). Standardized effect sizes ranged from $b_{stand} = .265$ for intrinsic motivation between T3 and T4 to $b_{stand} = .956$ for self-regulated learning from T1 to T2.

Cross-Lagged Effects

The cross-lagged effects represent the unique influence of one variable at a time point to another variable at the next time point, while controlling for the autoregressive effects and all other cross-lagged effects in the model (Selig & Little, 2012).

For autonomy, no effects across time were significant. Competence showed a moderate negative effect on autonomy from T1 to T2 ($b_{stand} = -.253$, $p = .003$) and a small positive effect from T2 to T3 ($b_{stand} = .146$, $p = .024$). Social

Table 1. Correlations of all variables

Scale name	Autonomy	Competence	Social relatedness	Intrinsic motivation	Self-regulated learning
T1 (lower triangle) and T2 (upper triangle)					
Autonomy	—	.445	.176	.478	.107
Competence	.626	—	.271	.640	.104
Social relatedness	.198	.272	—	.273	.174
Intrinsic motivation	.609	.641	.232	—	.150
Self-regulated learning	.120	.091	.174	.124	—
T3 (lower triangle) and T4 (upper triangle)					
Autonomy	—	.458	.247	.401	.138
Competence	.518	—	.397	.560	.120
Social relatedness	.302	.391	—	.324	.178
Intrinsic motivation	.562	.610	.377	—	.165
Self-regulated learning	.137	.133	.191	.220	—

Note. All effects are significant at the $p < .01$ level.

relatedness exhibited a small negative effect on self-regulated learning from T3 to T4 ($b_{stand} = -.102$, $p = .042$). Intrinsic motivation showed a small positive effect on autonomy ($b_{stand} = .127$, $p = .013$) and a small negative effect on social relatedness ($b_{stand} = -.098$, $p = .009$) from T1 to T2. Furthermore, intrinsic motivation also exhibited a moderate negative effect on perceived competence ($b_{stand} = -.212$, $p = .006$) and self-regulated learning ($b_{stand} = -.190$, $p = .023$) between T3 and T4. Finally, self-regulated learning positively predicted perceived competence from T3 to T4 ($b_{stand} = .136$, $p = .013$) and intrinsic motivation at all time points, albeit with small effect sizes (T1 → T2: $b_{stand} = .083$, $p = .005$; T2 → T3: $b_{stand} = .094$, $p = .009$; T3 → T4: $b_{stand} = .115$, $p = .030$).

Exploratory Analysis – T1 to T2

As reported, our analyses did not reveal the expected effects, particularly regarding the impact of basic psychological need satisfaction on intrinsic motivation. We therefore conducted an additional exploratory analysis including only T1 and T4 to eliminate the potential influence of varying time intervals between the first three measurement time points and the third and fourth measurement time points.

The model fits the data well [$\chi^2(463) = 1,706.397$, $p < .001$; CFI = .956; TLI = .947; RMSEA = .029 [.027, .030]; SRMR = .053]. Unstandardized and standardized effects are reported in Tables S8 and S9 in the Supplementary Material. In summary, a similar pattern of effects could be observed in comparison to the main analysis. All autoregressive effects remained significant (with standardized effect sizes ranging from $b_{stand} = .167$ for intrinsic motivation to $b_{stand} = .777$ for self-regulated learning). Moreover, the satisfaction of autonomy and social relatedness still showed no significant effects on intrinsic motivation. However, there was a medium-sized positive effect of competence on intrinsic motivation ($b_{stand} = .243$). No significant effects of intrinsic motivation on self-regulated learning could be observed. The effect of self-regulated learning on intrinsic motivation was slightly higher ($b_{stand} = .154$) than in the analysis including all four time points (where the effects were $b_{stand} = .083$ from T1 to T2 and $b_{stand} = .115$ from T3 to T4).

The largest differences could be observed for the patterns between the basic psychological need satisfaction and for the effects of intrinsic motivation on basic need satisfaction. Here, the negative effects of competence on autonomy (T1→T2) and social relatedness on self-regulated learning (T3→T4) disappeared, whereas autonomy now showed a negative effect on competence with $b_{stand} = -.294$. Additionally, all effects of intrinsic motivation on basic psychological need satisfaction observed in the original analysis were nonsignificant. Finally, self-regulated learning affected autonomy ($b_{stand} = .134$) and competence ($b_{stand} = .139$) in addition to intrinsic motivation.

Discussion

In our study, we investigated the association, reciprocal, and directional effects between higher education students' basic need satisfaction, intrinsic motivation, and self-regulated learning during emergency distance learning in times of COVID-19. We hypothesized that the satisfaction of the three basic psychological needs would be positively related to intrinsic motivation at each time point. Furthermore, we were interested in directional and reciprocal effects between the investigated constructs, specifically whether the satisfaction of the three basic psychological needs at one time point effects intrinsic motivation at the next time point and which role self-regulated learning played for intrinsic motivation and vice versa.

Cross-Sectional Relationships Between Basic Psychological Need Satisfaction, Intrinsic Motivation, and Self-Regulated Learning

As hypothesized, all three basic psychological needs were positively related to intrinsic motivation at all time points on a cross-sectional level, with social relatedness showing the smallest and perceived competence the largest effects. These results could be observed in the main cross-lagged panel model and in the additional explorative analysis including only T1 and T4. They are also in line with previous research (Bureau et al., 2021) and the theoretical assumptions of self-determination theory (Ryan & Deci, 2020). However, our study extends previous research to the emergency distance learning context, underlining SDT's claim of universality. Moreover, basic psychological needs satisfaction was positively related to self-regulated learning at all time points, albeit with small to moderate effects. Nevertheless, our findings emphasize the importance of basic psychological need satisfaction for student motivation and learning. Considering possible upcoming crises, it therefore seems to be particularly important to prioritize support for the satisfaction of basic psychological needs on both the institutional and individual levels. For example, on an institutional level, programs can be implemented that enable contact between students also in the virtual space. At the same time, training courses can be offered for university teachers, in which the importance of basic psychological need and possible ways of promoting them in teaching are conveyed.

Directional Effects of Basic Need Satisfaction on Intrinsic Motivation

Regarding the cross-lagged effects of the three basic psychological needs on intrinsic motivation, no significant effects could be found. Thus, in our study, although perceived competence, autonomy, and social relatedness were indeed cross-sectionally correlated at each time point, their predictive power across time was not as expected. This is particularly interesting as SDT clearly states that perceived competence, autonomy, and social relatedness are prerequisites for intrinsic motivation (Ryan & Deci, 2020). Moreover, the satisfaction of basic psychological needs has led to longer-lasting positive effects in other contexts and is therefore recognized as an important factor in resilience (e.g., Carmona-Halty et al., 2019).

Our findings suggest that the satisfaction of the basic psychological needs must be maintained continuously to have a positive impact on the motivation and learning behavior of students. Therefore, university teachers need to be aware that supporting competence, autonomy, and social relatedness must be a fixed element in the classroom.

However, it is possible that our results were influenced by other factors as well. Statistically, our model tested for the unique effect of each construct while controlling for all other incorporated constructs. Garn and colleagues (2019) suggest that a general basic need satisfaction factor may have stronger predictive power than testing the unique contribution of each basic need on its own, which would also be consistent with the assumption of SDT that the satisfaction of all three basic psychological needs is essential for the emergence and maintenance of autonomous motivation (Deci & Ryan, 2000). In our study, we have modeled the three basic needs as individual latent variables to identify the respective contribution of perceived competence, autonomy, and social relatedness to intrinsic motivation. However, future research could pursue the approach of a general factor to see if, indeed, all three basic needs must be considered together to increase intrinsic motivation. Another explanation might be that in our study, we also focused on basic need satisfaction or a lack thereof. However, recently, need frustration has been investigated as a distinct construct alongside need satisfaction (Vansteenkiste et al., 2020). Conceptualized as an "active threat of the psychological needs" (Vansteenkiste et al., 2020, p. 9), need frustration has proven to have a unique influence on motivation and well-being above and beyond the lack of need satisfaction. Given the life-changing experience of living through a global pandemic with its restrictions of personal freedom, fear of infection and overall change in daily life may have not only led to a lack of need satisfaction but, indeed, a frustration of basic psychological needs. More research would be needed to explore the unique effects of basic need frustration in particularly challenging and uncertain situations.

The Role of Self-Regulated Learning

Previous research failed to establish a clear directional effect between intrinsic motivation and self-regulated learning, with some studies showing self-regulated learning as a precursor of motivation (Ning & Downing, 2010), while others found self-regulated learning to be predicted by motivation (Mukhtar et al., 2018). In our study, self-regulated learning consistently showed a small but significant positive effect on intrinsic motivation across all time points. This effect increased when only considering T1 and T4 in our exploratory analysis.

This finding points to the relevance of self-regulated learning in higher education when external regulation mechanisms such as on-site classes are suspended. Educators should focus on promoting self-regulated learning. This could involve providing student with prompts to set goals and plan and monitor their learning, giving regular feedback, and emphasize the importance of regular reflection. By promoting self-regulated learning, educators can help students become more engaged and motivated learners, which can improve their academic performance and achievement.

At the same time, intrinsic motivation did not have any significant effect on self-regulated learning between T1 and T2 and T2 and T3. Between T3 and T4, however, there was a small and significant negative effect, indicating that higher intrinsic motivation would lead to lower self-regulation. This is an unexpected result, as in previous studies, intrinsic motivation was positively related to self-regulated learning (Mukhtar et al., 2018). One possible explanation might be that highly intrinsically motivated students may use other methods at the expense of self-regulated learning or feel that they do not need to apply self-regulated learning to reach their goals. A person-centered approach might provide further insight into the development and codevelopment of self-regulated learning and intrinsic motivation.

Implications of the Present Study

Our study showed that although the satisfaction of the three psychological needs for autonomy, competence, and social relatedness had the expected positive effects on intrinsic motivation at each time point, persistent effects were observed neither within a relatively short time (T1 to T2 and T2 to T3) nor over a longer period (T3 to T4). Although the satisfaction of basic psychological needs has led to longer-lasting positive effects in other contexts and is therefore recognized as an important factor in resilience (e.g., Carmona-Halty et al., 2019), this was not supported by our study. Instructors should therefore strive to provide an environment conducive to ongoing need satisfaction even in distance learning.

In addition, self-regulated learning has been shown to play an important role in intrinsic motivation both short term and long term. Thus, instructing students on how to apply self-regulated learning strategies is a particularly worthwhile investment, as it can also have a positive long-term impact on intrinsic motivation.

Limitations and Strengths

One of the strengths of our study is its longitudinal design. Moreover, data collection started soon after the first lockdown in Austria and spanned over more than a year. Although our study was also not immune to the dropout common in longitudinal studies, the sample size remained large, and the applied statistical method of full information maximum likelihood allowed the use of all available data throughout all time points.

Given these strengths, we must also acknowledge several limitations. First, due to the circumstances, we utilized online self-reports. This self-selection led to an overrepresentation of female participants. Furthermore, to ensure a high level of anonymization, we did not ask for university affiliation and therefore cannot consider the clustering of students in universities. However, the measures to mitigate the virus were largely identical across all higher education institutions in Austria as they were mandated by the federal government, which presumably reduced the variation between students from different institutions. We also recognize that the elapsed time between T3 and T4 is longer than the time spans between the first three measurement points. Further studies may aim to equalize the timespan between the measurement points so that a clearer interpretation of developmental patterns might be possible.

Conclusion

Although the results of our cross-sectional analysis supported SDT's original postulate that basic need satisfaction has beneficial effects on intrinsic motivation, the results of the longitudinal analyses did not reveal directional effects over time when controlling for the prior levels of the other constructs. Our study expands previous knowledge on the longitudinal effects of the three basic psychological needs – perceived competence, autonomy, and social relatedness – on intrinsic motivation in the context of the pandemic-induced emergency distance learning. We furthermore extended previous research by including self-regulated learning as an important aspect in the context of distance learning in our model. Previous studies failed to establish whether self-regulated learning impacts intrinsic motivation or whether the directional relationship between the two constructs is reciprocal or even reversed. Our results speak in favor of a small but consistent positive effect of self-regulated learning on intrinsic motivation, drawing attention to the importance of self-regulated learning for motivation above and beyond basic psychological need satisfaction. On the contrary, intrinsic motivation had no or a small negative effect on self-regulated learning.

References

Bartholomew, K. J., Ntoumanis, N., Ryan, R. M., Bosch, J. A., & Thøgersen-Ntoumani, C. (2011). Self-determination theory and diminished functioning: The role of interpersonal control and psychological need thwarting. *Personality and Social Psychology Bulletin, 37*(11), 1459–1473. https://doi.org/10.1177/0146167211413125

Bozkurt, A., Jung, I., Xiao, J., Vladimirschi, V., Schuwer, R., Egorov, G., Lambert, S. R., Al-Freih, M., Pete, J., Olcott, D., Jr., Rodes, V., Aranciaga, I., Bali, M., Alvarez, Jr., Abel, V., Roberts, J., Pazurek, A., Raffaghelli, J. E., Panagiotou, N., de Coëtlogon, P., ... Paskevicius, M. (2020). A global outlook to the interruption of education due to COVID-19 pandemic: Navigating in a time of uncertainty and crisis. *Asian Journal of Distance Education, 15*(1), 1–126. https://doi.org/10.5281/zenodo.3878572

Broadbent, J., & Poon, W. L. (2015). Self-regulated learning strategies & academic achievement in online higher education learning environments: A systematic review. *The Internet and Higher Education, 27*, 1–13. https://doi.org/10.1016/j.iheduc.2015.04.007

Brown, T. A. (2015). *Confirmatory factor analysis for applied research* (2nd ed.). The Guilford Press.

Bureau, J. S., Howard, J. L., Chong, J. X. Y., & Guay, F. (2021). Pathways to student motivation: A meta-analysis of antecedents of autonomous and controlled motivations. *Review of Educational Research, 92*(1), Article 003465432110424. https://doi.org/10.3102/00346543211042426

Campbell, D. F. J., Pausits, A., & Reisky, F. (2022). Die Auswirkungen von COVID-19 auf die Lehre an Österreichs Hochschulen. Erste empirische Evidenzen und deren systematische Reflexion. *Zeitschrift für Hochschulrecht Hochschulmanagement und Hochschulpolitik zfhr, 21*(2), Article 55. https://doi.org/10.33196/zfhr202202005501

Carmona-Halty, M., Schaufeli, W. B., Llorens, S., & Salanova, M. (2019). Satisfaction of basic psychological needs leads to better academic performance via increased psychological capital: A three-wave longitudinal study among high school students. *Frontiers in Psychology, 10*, Article 2113. https://doi.org/10.3389/fpsyg.2019.02113

Chen, F. F. (2007). Sensitivity of goodness of fit indexes to lack of measurement invariance. *Structural Equation Modeling: A Multidisciplinary Journal, 14*(3), 464–504. https://doi.org/10.1080/10705510701301834

Corpus, J. H., Robinson, K. A., & Wormington, S. V. (2020). Trajectories of motivation and their academic correlates over the first year of college. *Contemporary Educational Psychology*, *63*, Article 101907. https://doi.org/10.1016/j.cedpsych.2020.101907

Cronbach, L. J., & Shavelson, R. J. (2004). My current thoughts on coefficient alpha and successor procedures. *Educational and Psychological Measurement*, *64*(3), 391–418. https://doi.org/10.1177/0013164404266386

Deci, E. L., & Ryan, R. M. (2000). The "What" and "Why" of goal pursuits: Human needs and the self-determination of behavior. *Psychological Inquiry*, *11*(4), 227–268. https://doi.org/10.1207/S15327965PLI1104_01

Farnell, T., Skledar Matijević, A., & Šćukanec Schmidt, N. (2021). *The impact of COVID-19 on higher education: A review of emerging evidence (NESET Report)*. Publications Office of the European Union. https://data.europa.eu/doi/10.2766/069216

Garn, A. C., Morin, A. J. S., & Lonsdale, C. (2019). Basic psychological need satisfaction toward learning: A longitudinal test of mediation using bifactor exploratory structural equation modeling. *Journal of Educational Psychology*, *111*(2), 354–372. https://doi.org/10.1037/edu0000283

Gignac, G. E., & Szodorai, E. T. (2016). Effect size guidelines for individual differences researchers. *Personality and Individual Differences*, *102*, 74–78. https://doi.org/10.1016/j.paid.2016.06.069

Hadwin, A. F., Sukhawathanakul, P., Rostampour, R., & Bahena-Olivares, L. M. (2022). Do self-regulated learning practices and intervention mitigate the impact of academic challenges and COVID-19 distress on academic performance during online learning? *Frontiers in Psychology*, *13*, Article 813529. https://doi.org/10.3389/fpsyg.2022.813529

Heissel, A., Pietrek, A., Flunger, B., Fydrich, T., Rapp, M. A., Heinzel, S., & Vansteenkiste, M. (2018). The validation of the German basic psychological need satisfaction and frustration scale in the context of mental health. *European Journal of Health Psychology*, *25*(4), 119–132. https://doi.org/10.1027/2512-8442/a000017

Hensley, L. C., Iaconelli, R., & Wolters, C. A. (2022). This weird time we're in": How a sudden change to remote education impacted college students' self-regulated learning. *Journal of Research on Technology in Education*, *54*(sup1), S203–S218. https://doi.org/10.1080/15391523.2021.1916414

Higgins, N. L., Rathner, J. A., & Frankland, S. (2021). Development of self-regulated learning: A longitudinal study on academic performance in undergraduate science. *Research in Science & Technological Education*, 1–25. https://doi.org/10.1080/02635143.2021.1997978

Holzer, J., Lüftenegger, M., Korlat, S., Pelikan, E., Salmela-Aro, K., Spiel, C., & Schober, B. (2021). Higher education in times of COVID-19: University students' basic need satisfaction, self-regulated learning, and well-being. *AERA Open*, *7*, Article 233285842110031. https://doi.org/10.1177/23328584211003164

Hsu, H.-C. K., Wang, C. V., & Levesque-Bristol, C. (2019). Reexamining the impact of self-determination theory on learning outcomes in the online learning environment. *Education and Information Technologies*, *24*(3), 2159–2174. https://doi.org/10.1007/s10639-019-09863-w

Hu, L., & Bentler, P. M. (1999). Cutoff criteria for fit indexes in covariance structure analysis: Conventional criteria versus new alternatives. *Structural Equation Modeling: A Multidisciplinary Journal*, *6*(1), 1–55. https://doi.org/10.1080/10705519909540118

Janke, S., Messerer, L. A. S., & Daumiller, M. (2022). Motivational development in times of campus closure: Longitudinal trends in undergraduate students' need satisfaction and intrinsic learning motivation. *British Journal of Educational Psychology*, *92*(4), 1582–1596. https://doi.org/10.1111/bjep.12522

Jeno, L. M., Nylehn, J., Hole, T. N., Raaheim, A., Velle, G., & Vandvik, V. (2023). Motivational determinants of students' academic functioning: The role of autonomy-support, autonomous motivation, and perceived competence. *Scandinavian Journal of Educational Research*, *67*(2), 194–211. https://doi.org/10.1080/00313831.2021.1990125

Karimi, S., & Sotoodeh, B. (2020). The mediating role of intrinsic motivation in the relationship between basic psychological needs satisfaction and academic engagement in agriculture students. *Teaching in Higher Education*, *25*(8), 959–975. https://doi.org/10.1080/13562517.2019.1623775

Kizilcec, R. F., Pérez-Sanagustín, M., & Maldonado, J. J. (2017). Self-regulated learning strategies predict learner behavior and goal attainment in Massive Open Online Courses. *Computers & Education*, *104*, 18–33. https://doi.org/10.1016/j.compedu.2016.10.001

Klingsieck, K. B. (2018). Kurz und knapp – die Kurzskala des Fragebogens "Lernstrategien im Studium" (LIST). *Zeitschrift für Pädagogische Psychologie*, *32*(4), 249–259. https://doi.org/10.1024/1010-0652/a000230

Klingsieck, K. B., Fries, S., Horz, C., & Hofer, M. (2012). Procrastination in a distance university setting. *Distance Education*, *33*(3), 295–310. https://doi.org/10.1080/01587919.2012.723165

Kusurkar, R. A., Ten Cate, Th. J., Vos, C. M. P., Westers, P., & Croiset, G. (2013). How motivation affects academic performance: A structural equation modelling analysis. *Advances in Health Sciences Education*, *18*(1), 57–69. https://doi.org/10.1007/s10459-012-9354-3

Little, R. J. A. (1988). A test of missing completely at random for multivariate data with missing values. *Journal of the American Statistical Association*, *83*(404), 1198–1202. https://doi.org/10.1080/01621459.1988.10478722

Little, T. D., Preacher, K. J., Selig, J. P., & Card, N. A. (2007). New developments in latent variable panel analyses of longitudinal data. *International Journal of Behavioral Development*, *31*(4), 357–365. https://doi.org/10.1177/0165025407077757

Lüdtke, O., Robitzsch, A., Trautwein, U., & Köller, O. (2007). Umgang mit fehlenden Werten in der psychologischen Forschung. *Psychologische Rundschau*, *58*(2), 103–117. https://doi.org/10.1026/0033-3042.58.2.103

Mukhtar, F., Muis, K., & Elizov, M. (2018). Relations between psychological needs satisfaction, motivation, and self-regulated learning strategies in medical residents: A cross-sectional study [version 1]. *MedEdPublish*, *7*(87). https://doi.org/10.15694/mep.2018.0000087.1

Müller, F. H., & Palekčić, M. (2005). Continuity of motivation in higher education: A three-year follow-up study. *Review of Psychology*, *12*(1), 31–43

Ning, H. K., & Downing, K. (2010). The reciprocal relationship between motivation and self-regulation: A longitudinal study on academic performance. *Learning and Individual Differences*, *20*(6), 682–686. https://doi.org/10.1016/j.lindif.2010.09.010

Noyens, D., Donche, V., Coertjens, L., van Daal, T., & Van Petegem, P. (2019). The directional links between students' academic motivation and social integration during the first year of higher education. *European Journal of Psychology of Education*, *34*(1), 67–86. https://doi.org/10.1007/s10212-017-0365-6

Ntoumanis, N., Ng, J. Y. Y., Prestwich, A., Quested, E., Hancox, J. E., Thøgersen-Ntoumani, C., Deci, E. L., Ryan, R. M., Lonsdale, C., & Williams, G. C. (2021). A meta-analysis of self-determination theory-informed intervention studies in the health domain: Effects on motivation, health behavior, physical, and psychological health. *Health Psychology Review*, *15*(2), 214–244. https://doi.org/10.1080/17437199.2020.1718529

Pan, Y., & Gauvain, M. (2012). The continuity of college students' autonomous learning motivation and its predictors: A three-year longitudinal study. *Learning and Individual Differences*, *22*(1), 92–99. https://doi.org/10.1016/j.lindif.2011.11.010

Pelikan, E., Reiter, J., Bergen, K., Lüftenegger, M., Holzer, J., Korlat, S., Schober, B., & Spiel, C. (2022). Lernen unter COVID-19 Bedingungen: Zur Situation der Studierenden in Österreich. In H. Angenent, J. Petri, & T. Zimenkova (Eds.), *Bildungsforschung* (1. Aufl., Bd. 9, S. 200–215). transcript Verlag. https://doi.org/10.14361/9783839459843-013

Pelikan, E. R., Grützmacher, L., Holzer, J., Korlat, S., & Lüftenegger, M. (2023). *Supplementary materials to "The role of basic need satisfaction for motivation and self-regulated learning during COVID-19: A longitudinal study"*. https://doi.org/10.17605/OSF.IO/KX4WU

Pelikan, E. R., Korlat, S., Reiter, J., Holzer, J., Mayerhofer, M., Schober, B., Spiel, C., Hamzallari, O., Uka, A., Chen, J., Välimäki, M., Puharić, Z., Anusionwu, K. E., Okocha, A. N., Zabrodskaja, A., Salmela-Aro, K., Käser, U., Schultze-Krumbholz, A., Wachs, S., ... Lüftenegger, M. (2021). Distance learning in higher education during COVID-19: The role of basic psychological needs and intrinsic motivation for persistence and procrastination—a multi-country study. *PLoS ONE*, *16*(10), Article e0257346. https://doi.org/10.1371/journal.pone.0257346

Rodrigues, F., Macedo, R., Teixeira, D. S., Cid, L., Travassos, B., Neiva, H., & Monteiro, D. (2021). The co-occurrence of satisfaction and frustration of basic psychological needs and its relationship with exercisers' motivation. *The Journal of Psychology*, *155*(2), 165–185. https://doi.org/10.1080/00223980.2020.1862738

Rutkowski, L., & Svetina, D. (2014). Assessing the hypothesis of measurement invariance in the context of large-scale international surveys. *Educational and Psychological Measurement*, *74*(1), 31–57. https://doi.org/10.1177/0013164413498257

Ryan, R. M., & Deci, E. L. (2020). Intrinsic and extrinsic motivation from a self-determination theory perspective: Definitions, theory, practices, and future directions. *Contemporary Educational Psychology*, *61*, Article 101860. https://doi.org/10.1016/j.cedpsych.2020.101860

Ryan, R. M., Soenens, B., & Vansteenkiste, M. (2019). Reflections on self-determination theory as an organizing framework for personality psychology: Interfaces, integrations, issues, and unfinished business. *Journal of Personality*, *87*(1), 115–145. https://doi.org/10.1111/jopy.12440

Satorra, A., & Bentler, P. M. (1994). Corrections to test statistics and standard errors in covariance structure analysis. In A. von Eye & C. C. Clogg (Eds.), *Latent variables analysis: Applications for developmental research* (pp. 399–419). Sage Publications

Schober, B., Lüftenegger, M., & Spiel, C. (2021). *Learning conditions during COVID-19 Students (SUF edition)* [Data set]. AUSSDA. https://doi.org/10.11587/XIU3TX

Selig, J. P., & Little, T. D. (2012). Autoregressive and cross-lagged panel analysis for longitudinal data. In B. Laursen, T. D. Little, & N. A. Card (Eds.), *Handbook of developmental research methods* (pp. 265–278). The Guilford Press.

Thomas, A. E., Müller, F. H., & Bieg, S. (2018). Entwicklung und Validierung der Skalen zur motivationalen Regulation beim Lernen im Studium (SMR-LS). *Diagnostica*, *64*(3), 145–155. https://doi.org/10.1026/0012-1924/a000201

Trigueros, R., Aguilar-Parra, J. M., Cangas-Díaz, A. J., Fernández-Batanero, J. M., Mañas, M. A., Arias, V. B., & López-Liria, R. (2019). The influence of the trainer on the motivation and resilience of sportspeople: A study from the perspective of self-determination theory. *PLoS ONE*, *14*(8), Article e0221461. https://doi.org/10.1371/journal.pone.0221461

Van den Broeck, A., Ferris, D. L., Chang, C.-H., & Rosen, C. C. (2016). A review of self-determination theory's basic psychological needs at work. *Journal of Management*, *42*(5), 1195–1229. https://doi.org/10.1177/0149206316632058

Vansteenkiste, M., Ryan, R. M., & Soenens, B. (2020). Basic psychological need theory: Advancements, critical themes, and future directions. *Motivation and Emotion*, *44*(1), 1–31. https://doi.org/10.1007/s11031-019-09818-1

Zhang, T., Taub, M., & Chen, Z. (2021). *Measuring the impact of COVID-19 induced campus closure on student self-regulated learning in physics online learning modules*. LAK21: 11th International Learning Analytics and Knowledge Conference (pp.110–120). https://doi.org/10.1145/3448139.3448150

Zimmerman, B. J. (2000). Chapter 2—Attaining self-regulation: A social cognitive perspective. In M. Boekaerts, P. R. Pintrich, & M. Zeidner (Eds.), *Handbook of self-regulation* (pp. 13–39). Academic Press. https://doi.org/10.1016/B978-012109890-2/50031-7

History

Received August 9, 2022
Revision received March 17, 2023
Accepted March 18, 2023
Published online July 18, 2023

Publication Ethics

The Austrian Federal Ministry of Education, Science, and Research recommended participation in the study on their website. Prior to data collection, participants were informed about the study's goals and inclusion criteria (attending a higher education institution in Austria). Participation was voluntary. At the end of the first survey, students were invited to participate in the longitudinal study. If they approved, they were contacted via e-mail for subsequent measurement points. Only data from students who gave active consent were included in the data set. Data analysis was conducted with anonymized data.

Authorship

Elisabeth R. Pelikan: conceptualization, formal analysis, investigation, methodology, writing – original draft, writing – review & editing. Luisa Grützmacher: methodology, formal analysis, writing – review & editing. Katharina Hager: writing – original draft, writing – review & editing. Julia Holzer: conceptualization, investigation, writing – review & editing. Selma Korlat: conceptualization, project administration, data curation, investigation, project administration, writing – review & editing. Martin Mayerhofer: data curation, writing – review & editing. Barbara Schober: conceptualization, funding acquisition. Christiane Spiel: conceptualization, funding acquisition. Marko Lüftenegger: conceptualization, funding acquisition, supervision, writing – review & editing. All authors approved the final version of the article.

Open Data

The supplementary materials and data are available in OSF at https://doi.org/10.17605/OSF.IO/KX4WU (Pelikan et al., 2023).

Funding

This work has been funded by the Vienna Science and Technology Fund (WWTF, grant ID: 10.47379/EICOV20025), by MEGA Bildungsstiftung, and the City of Vienna.

ORCID

Elisabeth Rosa Pelikan
 https://orcid.org/0000-0003-2317-9237
Luisa Grützmacher
 https://orcid.org/0000-0002-2384-1588
Julia Holzer
 https://orcid.org/0000-0002-0029-3291
Martin Mayerhofer
 https://orcid.org/0000-0002-2978-4385
Marko Lüftenegger
 https://orcid.org/0000-0001-8112-976X

Elisabeth R. Pelikan
Department of Developmental and Educational Psychology
University of Vienna
Universitätsstraße 7
1010 Vienna
Austria
elisabeth.pelikan@univie.ac.at

Erratum

Correction to Christiansen & Lueken, 2023

The article entitled "Lessons Learned: A Summary of Studies on Psychological Effects of the COVID-19 Pandemic" by Hanna Christiansen and Ulrike Lueken (*Zeitschrift für Psychologie*, *231*(2), 81–82. https://doi.org/10.1027/2151-2604/a000517) has now been published with the correct email address of its corresponding author.

The following email address has now been replaced:

Hanna Christiansen
christih@staff.uni-marburg.de

Reference

Christiansen, H., & Lueken, U. (2023). Lessons learned: A summary of studies on psychological effects of the COVID-19 pandemic. *Zeitschrift für Psychologie*, *231*(2), 81–82. https://doi.org/10.1027/2151-2604/a000517

Published online July 18, 2023

Instructions to Authors

The *Zeitschrift für Psychologie* publishes high-quality research from all branches of empirical psychology that is clearly of international interest and relevance, and does so in four topical issues per year. Each topical issue is carefully compiled by guest editors. The subjects being covered are determined by the editorial team after consultation within the scientific community, thus ensuring topicality. The *Zeitschrift für Psychologie* thus brings convenient, cutting-edge compilations of the best of modern psychological science, each covering an area of current interest.

***Zeitschrift für Psychologie* publishes the following types of articles:** Review Articles, Original Articles, Research Spotlights, Horizons, and Opinions.

Manuscript submission: A call for papers is issued for each topical issue. Current calls are available on the journal's website at http://www.hgf.io/zfp. Manuscripts should be submitted as Word or RTF documents by e-mail to the responsible guest editor(s). An article can only be considered for publication in the *Zeitschrift für Psychologie* if it can be assigned to one of the topical issues that have been announced. The journal does not accept general submissions.

Detailed instructions to authors are provided at **http://www.hgf.io/zfp**

Copyright Agreement: By submitting an article, the author confirms and guarantees on behalf of themselves and any co-authors that he or she holds all copyright in and titles to the submitted contribution, including any figures, photographs, line drawings, plans, maps, sketches and tables, and that the article and its contents do not infringe in any way on the rights of third parties. The author indemnifies and holds harmless the publisher from any third-party claims. The author agrees, upon acceptance of the article for publication, to transfer to the publisher on behalf of themselves and any coauthors the exclusive right to reproduce and distribute the article and its contents, both physically and in nonphysical, electronic, and other form, in the journal to which it has been submitted and in other independent publications, with no limits on the number of copies or on the form or the extent of the distribution. These rights are transferred for the duration of copyright as defined by international law. Furthermore, the author transfers to the publisher the following exclusive rights to the article and its contents:

1. The rights to produce advance copies, reprints, or offprints of the article, in full or in part, to undertake or allow translations into other languages, to distribute other forms or modified versions of the article, and to produce and distribute summaries or abstracts.
2. The rights to microfilm and microfiche editions or similar, to the use of the article and its contents in videotext, teletext, and similar systems, to recordings or reproduction using other media, digital or analog, including electronic, magnetic, and optical media, and in multimedia form, as well as for public broadcasting in radio, television, or other forms of broadcast.
3. The rights to store the article and its content in machine-readable or electronic form on all media (such as computer disks, compact disks, magnetic tape), to store the article and its contents in online databases belonging to the publisher or third parties for viewing or downloading by third parties, and to present or reproduce the article or its contents on visual display screens, monitors, and similar devices, either directly or via data transmission.
4. The rights to reproduce and distribute the article and its contents by all other means, including photomechanical and similar processes (such as photocopying or facsimile), and as part of so-called document delivery services.
5. The right to transfer any or all rights mentioned in this agreement, as well as rights retained by the relevant copyright clearing centers, including royalty rights to third parties.

Online Rights for Journal Articles: Guidelines on authors' rights to archive electronic versions of their manuscripts online are given in the document "Guidelines on sharing and use of articles in Hogrefe journals" on the journal's web page at http://www.hgf.io/zfp

August 2021